weekend **crochet** for babies

Sue Whiting

weekend **crochet** for babies

*24 cute crochet designs,
from sweaters and jackets
to hats and toys*

TRAFALGAR SQUARE
North Pomfret, Vermont

First published in 2008 by
Trafalgar Square Books
North Pomfret, VT 05053

Library of Congress Control Number:
2008932403
ISBN 978-1-57076-423-3

Senior Editor: Clare Sayer
Production: Laurence Poos
Photography: Sian Irvine and
Paul Bricknell
Design: Lucy Parissi
Pattern checking: Sue Horan
Stitch diagrams: Kuo Kang Chen
Illustrations: Carrie Hill
Editorial Direction: Rosemary Wilkinson

10 9 8 7 6 5 4 3 2 1

Reproduction by Modern Age Repro,
Hong Kong
Printed and bound by Craft Print
International, Singapore

contents

introduction

Making something for a new arrival is both rewarding and fun. And, when you choose to crochet that special item, it can be quick too! Here you will find a lovely collection of quick and easy designs to delight any new baby—or their mother, all of which can be completed in one or two weekends. All the patterns cater for tiny babies up to toddlers so you can make them for their big sister or brother too!

How to crochet

It's not difficult to learn to crochet—especially if you are already a knitter and are familiar with handling yarn and knitting needles. Crochet only uses a hook, not a pair of needles, and there is only ever one stitch on the hook at any time. This makes it much more versatile and greatly reduces the chances of dropping stitches! Crochet has a few stitches to learn but, as these are all variations on a theme, you'll find it really easy to master them. Once you've got the hang of one stitch, you'll find it really easy to pick up the others.

WHAT YOU NEED

To crochet something you don't need a lot of equipment. You just need a pattern—you've got those in this book—and a few other simple things. And the pattern will tell you exactly what these are.

Your pattern will tell you how much and what type of yarn you need to buy, and what size crochet hook to use. Crochet hooks come in lots of different sizes and there are different ways these sizes are measured—metric, american and imperial. Opposite is a chart that shows you the equivalent sizes in each measurement system.

Your pattern will also tell you if you need anything else—like buttons or ribbon. Apart from these few things, there's not much else you need! A pair of scissors will obviously be useful for cutting the yarn, and a tape measure will help you check the crocheted pieces are the right size. You will probably have to sew up a few seams, or darn in a few yarn ends—so you'll need a blunt-pointed needle with a large eye. Like those used for tapestry or sewing up knitted things, this sort of needle is not only easy to thread with a thick yarn but also the blunt "point" slips between the strands of yarn and makes sewing up neat and easy.

SIZING

All the designs in this book can be made for babies from newborn up to 18 months old. Although approximate ages are given, it's a much better idea to choose the size you want to make by measuring the actual chest size of the child. If you are still unsure what size to choose, compare the actual measurements of the garment—given at the start of the pattern—with those of a something you know fits the child well.

CROCHET HOOK CONVERSION CHART

METRIC	USA	IMPERIAL (old UK)
2.00 mm	B1	14
2.25 mm	B1	13
2.50 mm	C2	12
3.00 mm	D3	11
3.25 mm	D3	10
3.50 mm	E4	9
3.75 mm	F5	–
4.00 mm	G6	8
4.50 mm	7	7
5.00 mm	H8	6
5.50 mm	I9	5
6.00 mm	J10	4
6.50 mm	K10½	3
7.00 mm	(no equivalent)	2
8.00 mm	L11	0
9.00 mm	13	00
10.00 mm	N15	000

YARNS

Almost any knitting yarn can be used for crochet but, when making items for little ones, you need to bear a few things in mind. Choose yarns that are soft and gentle against a baby's skin. Most of the yarns are featured in this book are machine washable.

Colinette Jitterbug 100% merino wool, 318 yd/291 m per 4 oz (110 g) hank, machine washable (cold wool cycle), tumble dry (low setting).

Colinette Banyan 49% cotton, 51% viscose, 112 yd/102 m per 1¾ oz (50 g) hank, hand wash.

Colinette Prism 50% wool, 50% cotton, 131 yd/120 m per 3½ oz (100 g) hank, hand wash.

Rowan RYC Cashsoft DK (and **Cashsoft Baby DK**) 57% extra fine merino, 33% microfiber, 10% cashmere, 142 yd/130 m per 1¾ oz (50 g) ball, machine washable (wool cycle).

Rowan Pure Wool DK 100% superwash wool, 137 yd/125 m per 1¾ oz (50 g) ball, machine washable (wool cycle).

Rowan Wool Cotton 50% merino wool, 50% cotton, 123 yd/113 m per 1¾ oz (50 g) ball, machine washable (wool cycle).

Rowan Tapestry 70% wool, 30% soybean protein fiber, 131 yd/120 m per 1¾ oz (50 g) ball, hand wash.

Rowan Handknit Cotton DK 100% cotton, 93 yd/85 m per 1¾ oz (50 g) ball, machine washable (wool cycle).

Rowan Calmer 75% cotton, 25% acrylic microfiber, 175 yd/160 m per 1¾ oz (50 g) ball, hand wash.

Rowan All Seasons Cotton 60% cotton, 40% acrylic microfiber, 98 yd/90 m per 1¾ oz (50 g) ball, machine washable (wool cycle).

Rowan Kid Classic 70% lambswool, 26% kid mohair, 4% nylon, 153 yd/140 m per 1¾ oz (50 g) ball, hand wash.

Rowan Kidsilk Aura 75% kid mohair, 25% silk, 82 yd/75 m per 1 oz (25 g) ball, hand wash.

Rowan Cocoon 80% merino wool, 20% kid mohair, 126 yd/115 m per 3½ oz (100 g) ball, hand wash.

Rowan Big Wool 100% merino wool, 87 yd/80 m per 3½ oz (100 g) ball, hand wash.

Twilleys Freedom Spirit 100% wool, 131 yd/120 m per 1¾ oz (50 g) ball, hand wash.

ABBREVIATIONS

All crochet patterns are written in a sort of shorthand—all the "technical" terms are shortened, or abbreviated, to just a few letters. These abbreviations are standard to almost all crochet patterns and here you've got a full list of all the ones you need for the designs in this book. Sometimes there will be a special stitch, or stitch group, used for one particular design only—if this is the case that special abbreviation will appear with the pattern it's needed for.

GAUGE

The size of a finished piece of crochet is controlled by how big, or small, the stitches and rows are, and the term used to describe this is the "gauge." Because the gauge governs the size of the finished item and the amount of yarn you will need, it's really important you crochet at the correct gauge.

To check your gauge, make a small square of crochet in the stitch used for the garment, using the yarn and the size of hook given in the pattern. Make sure this gauge swatch is at least 6 in (15 cm) square so that you can easily count the number of stitches and rows on it.

Once you've completed the crochet square, mark out with pins the number of stitches the gauge section of the pattern states there should be to 4 in (10 cm). Measure the distance between the pins—if this measurement is 4 in (10 cm) your gauge is correct and you are safe to make the garment using that size crochet hook.

If the distance between the pins is less than 4 in (10 cm), you are crocheting too tight and you need to make another swatch using a bigger crochet hook. And if the measurement is more than it should be, your crochet is too loose and you will need to use a smaller hook.

Check your row gauge is correct in the same way. Once you've worked out what size hook you need to use, use this size of hook for the garment instead of the size stated in the pattern. If other sizes of hook are needed, you'll need to adjust the size you use here too—if you've used one size smaller hook to get the gauge required, use one size smaller hook than stated for all the other hooks you need too.

CROCHET ABBREVIATIONS

alt – alternate

beg – beginning

ch – chain

cont – continue

dc – double crochet

dc2tog – (insert hook as indicated, yo and draw loop through) twice, yo and draw through all 3 loops on hook

dec – decreas(e)(ing)

dtr – double treble

foll – following

hdc – half double crochet

inc – increas(e)(ing)

patt – pattern

rem – remain(ing)

rep – repeat

RS – right side

sc – single crochet

sp(s) – space(s)

sl st – slip stitch

st(s) – stitch(es)

tr – treble crochet

trtr – triple treble

tr2tog – (yo and insert hook as indicated, yo and draw loop through, yo and draw through 2 loops) twice, yo and draw through all 3 loops on hook

yo – yarn over hook

WS – wrong side

0 – no sts, times or rows to be worked for this size

cm – centimeters

in – inches

mm – millimeters

FOLLOWING A PATTERN

All the garments in this book are in more than one size, and the different figures needed for each size are given as a string of figures inside square brackets [ ]. Where only one set of figures is given, this refers to all sizes.

The information inside the round brackets ( ) should be repeated the number of times given after the brackets.

The amount of yarn the pattern says you will need is based on an average requirement and if you alter the length you may need more or less yarn. Each pattern has been designed to work in the yarn stated—and it may not work correctly if any other yarn is used.

The pattern gives details of the order in which you should crochet the different pieces that go together to make up the completed item. This order should be followed as often a later piece will need you to refer back to the size of a previous section, or some pieces need to have already been completed in order to add an edging or band.

COMPLETING THE GARMENT

Once all the main pieces have been crocheted, the garment can be sewn together. It's often a good idea to press the sections first. This is much easier to do before they are sewn up—especially with small pieces like those that make up a baby garment. You should find all the information you need to press the pieces on the ball band but, if in any doubt, it is usually safe to press the pieces carefully on the wrong side using a warm iron and covering the work with a damp cloth. However, if you are using a totally synthetic yarn, use a cool iron and a dry cloth! Allow all the pieces to cool down and dry naturally before sewing them together.

With each pattern in this book there is a little diagram that shows you the shape each main crocheted piece should be when it is completed. Use these as a guide to what shape your work should be once pressed.

The crocheted pieces can be joined together in 3 ways—by back stitching the seams, over sewing the seams or by crocheting the edges together. Whatever type of seam you decide to work, use the same yarn for the seam as used for the crochet and, in the case of sewn seams, a blunt-pointed sewing-up needle.

Back stitching a seam

This type of seam gives quite a bulky seam on the inside of the garment but can be useful if the edge isn't totally straight, or to join shoulder seams.

To back stitch a seam, hold the 2 edges to be joined right sides together and work a line of back stitch as close to the edge as you can, working each stitch through both layers of the crochet.

Over sewing a seam

This gives a totally flat seam and it's a good idea to use this type of seam to join side and sleeve seams.

To over sew a seam, hold the 2 edges to be joined with their right sides together and simply over sew along the edge, working each stitch through both layers. Once the seam is complete and the sections are opened out, you should find this type of seam is virtually invisible and almost totally flat.

Crocheting a seam

This type of seam is a good choice for seams like shoulder seams as it is as elastic as the crochet is and will not split when the garment is put on or taken off.

To crochet a seam, hold the two edges to be joined with their right sides together and attach the yarn at one end of the seam. Using the same size crochet hook as used for the main sections, work a row of single crochet along the edge, working each stitch through both layers.

If there are any buttons, ribbons or trims to be added to a garment it is very important these are very securely attached so there is no risk of them coming off. Babies and toddlers put everything they can in their mouths, and they could easily choke on a button!

THE CROCHET STITCHES

Crochet is very simple and basically consists of just a few different types of stitch.

Starting the work

Before you start any crochet, you need to make your first stitch. To make this first stitch, make a slip knot by forming the yarn end into a loop and hooking the ball end of the yarn through this loop (**fig. A**).

Gently pull on the free end of the yarn (not the end leading to the ball) to tighten this first stitch around the body of the hook. You are now ready to make the next lot of stitches. All the following stitches should be worked using the length of yarn that leads to the ball, leaving the free (cut) end of the yarn to be used to sew a seam later if required (**fig. B**).

FIGURE A   **FIGURE B**

Chain (ch)

A crochet chain is often used as the base for all the following stitches but it can also be used within a stitch pattern.

To make a chain stitch, take the yarn end that leads to the ball over the crochet hook, wrapping it over, in front and under the hook. Now draw this loop through the loop on the hook to make the chain stitch (**fig. C**). Continue in this way until the required number of chain stitches have been completed.

FIGURE C

Single crochet (sc)

This is possibly the most basic of crochet stitches. To make a single crochet, insert the hook into the work. Wrap the yarn around the hook in the same way as for a chain stitch. Draw this new loop through the work—you should now have 2 loops on the hook (**fig. D**). Wrap the yarn around the hook again and draw this new loop through both the loops on the hook to complete the stitch (**fig. E**).

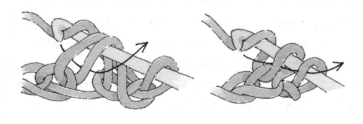

FIGURE D   **FIGURE E**

Double crochet (dc)

This is the other most commonly used crochet stitch. It's taller than a single crochet and therefore the work will grow faster if it's made up of double crochet stitches.

To make a double crochet, start by wrapping the yarn around the hook before inserting it into the work (**fig. F**). Wrap the yarn around the hook again and draw this new loop through just the

work, leaving 3 loops on the hook. Now wrap the yarn around the hook again (**fig. G**). Draw this new loop through just the first 2 loops on the hook. There are now just 2 loops left on the hook. Wrap the yarn around the hook once more (**fig. H**). Draw this new loop through both of the loops on the hook to complete the treble (**fig. J**).

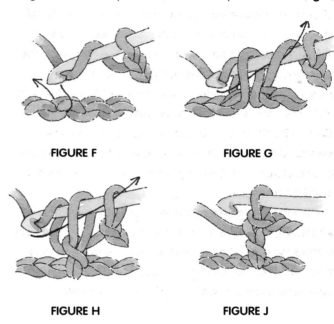

FIGURE F   **FIGURE G**

FIGURE H   **FIGURE J**

Half double crochet (hdc)

This type of stitch is taller than a single crochet but shorter than a double crochet and it's made in a similar way to a double crochet.

To make a half double crochet, wrap the yarn around the hook and insert it into the work. Wrap the yarn around the hook again and draw this new loop through the work, leaving 3 loops on the hook (**fig. K**). Wrap the yarn around the hook again and draw this new loop through all 3 loops on the hook to complete the half double (**fig. L**).

FIGURE K   **FIGURE L**

Treble crochet (tr)

This stitch is taller than a double. To make a treble, wrap the yarn twice around the hook before inserting it into the work. Wrap the yarn around the hook and draw this new loop through the work, leaving 4 loops on the hook. Wrap the yarn around the hook again. Draw this new loop through just the first 2 loops on the hook. There are now 3 loops left on the hook. Wrap the yarn around the hook once more. Draw this new loop through just the first 2 loops on the hook. There are now 2 loops on the hook. Wrap the yarn around the hook again. Draw this new loop through both of the loops on the hook to complete the treble crochet.

Taller stitches

Stitches that are taller than a treble can be worked in a similar way. For a double treble (dtr), wrap the yarn around the hook 3 times before inserting it into the work. Wrap the yarn around the hook and draw this new loop through the work. *Now wrap the yarn around the hook again and draw the new loop through just the first 2 loops on the hook. Repeat from * until there is only one loop left on the hook—the double treble is now completed.

Bigger trebles can also be made in this way—for each extra bit of height to the stitch, wrap the yarn around the hook once more before inserting it into the work (4 times for a qtr). Complete each bigger stitch in the same way—by drawing each new loop through just the first 2 loops on the hook until only one loop remains.

Slip stitch (sl st)

This stitch is often used to join sections or to move the crochet hook to another point to work the next set of stitches.

FIGURE M   **FIGURE N**

To make a slip stitch, insert the hook into the work. Wrap the yarn around the hook and draw this new loop through both the work and the loop on the hook to complete the slip stitch (**figs. M and N**).

PLACING THE STITCHES

Different crochet stitch patterns are often made up of the same sort of stitches but where these stitches are placed can alter the effect they create.

Working into the top of stitches

This is the standard way to place the next set of stitches and, unless a pattern says otherwise, this is how all the stitches should be worked.

Across the top of each crochet stitch is a little "V" formed by the yarn. Insert the hook through the work so that it slides under both of the bars that make up this "V" (**fig. O**).

FIGURE O
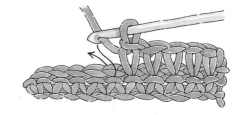

Working into chain stitches

As with all other crochet stitches, a chain stitch has a "V" of yarn on one side, with a third bar of yarn running across the back.

When working into a chain stitch, insert the hook through the center of the "V," picking up the underneath bar at the same time. This leaves just the front bar of the "V" not enclosed in the stitch (**fig. P**).

FIGURE P

Working into the front (or back) of a stitch

By picking up just the front (or back) bar of the "V" different effects can be created.

To work into the front loop (or bar) only, insert the hook through the work by sliding it under just the front bar that forms the "V," and thereby picking and enclosing just one strand of yarn in the stitch. The remaining bar of yarn that formed the "V" will sit on the surface of the work, forming a neat line across it (**fig. Q**).

FIGURE Q

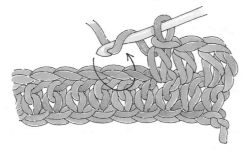

Working into the back loops (or bars) only in the same way will leave a line across the opposite side of the work (**fig. R**).

FIGURE R

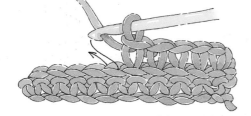

Working between stitches

Rather than working a new stitch into the top of the existing stitches, a new stitch can be worked between the stitches of the previous row. Obviously this is a lot easier to do if the previous stitches were tall stitches and it's easy to see where one stitch ends and the next stitch begins!

FIGURE S

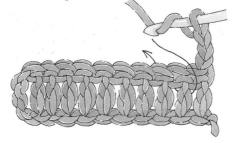

To work a stitch between the stitches of the previous row, simply insert the hook through the work between the "stalks" that make up the previous stitches. Working stitches in this way means you are not adding as much height to the work as you would if you were working into the top of them, and you are enclosing the strands of yarn that join the two stitches in this new stitch (**fig S**).

Working into chain spaces

A stitch pattern that is made of up lengths of chain between other crochet stitches will have what is termed a chain space (ch sp) underneath the length of chain stitches. To work into a chain space, simply insert the hook through this "hole" before wrapping the yarn around the hook to make the new stitch (**fig. T**).

FIGURE T

MAKING FABRICS

Crochet stitches can be joined together to make a crochet fabric in two ways—in rows, or in rounds.

Working in rows

Working backwards and forwards in rows of crochet stitches that all sit neatly on top of each other forms a flat fabric. Each row of new stitches is worked from the right towards the left. At the end of the row, the work is turned and the next row of stitches is again worked from right to left. At the beginning of each row, the working loop, and the hook, needs to be raised up to the height of the stitches that are to be used for this new row. To do this, a short length of chain—known as a turning chain—is made. The length of this chain varies depending on the type of stitch being worked. Sometimes this length of chain will take the place of the first stitch of the new row, sometimes it won't—but your pattern should tell you whether it does or not. If the turning chain does count as the first stitch of the row, you must work into the top chain stitch when working back across the stitches so that no accidental decreases are made and the number of stitches remains constant (**fig. V**).

FIGURE V

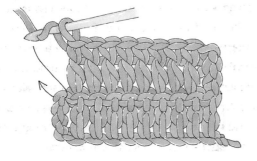

Working in rounds

As there is only ever one crochet stitch on the hook at any one time, it's really easy to work circular pieces of crochet by working round and round the work, instead of in rows. These circular pieces of crochet can form flat disks or tubes. Each new round of crochet is worked in the same sort of way as each new row of crochet, and at the beginning of each round there will be the turning chain. But, to join the end of each round to the beginning of it—and thereby form a tube or flat disk—the last stitch needs to be joined to the first stitch. Once all the stitches of the new round are complete, the ends are usually joined by working a slip stitch into the top of the turning chain (**fig. W**). When working in rounds of crochet there is no real need to turn the work at the end of each round. However, as crochet stitches look different on one side to the other, sometimes a pattern will tell you to turn the work after each round so that the required effect is created. If the pattern says "turn," then you should. If it doesn't, then don't!

FIGURE W

FASTENING OFF

Once a crochet section is completed, there will still be the one working loop—or stitch—on the hook.

To permanently fasten off this last stitch, cut the yarn about 4–5 in (10–12 cm) from the work. Take the yarn around the hook in the usual way and draw this cut end of yarn through the last stitch. Pull gently on the cut end to tighten the last stitch. Depending on how the pieces are to be joined together, cut the yarn so that a long end is left as this can be used to sew the seams.

SHAPING IN CROCHET

Obviously not all garments are made up of straight pieces of crochet, or shapeless tubes! So, at some point, you may need to increase or decreases stitches to make the piece the shape it should be.

There are lots of different ways this shaping can be worked and each method is more suited to one stitch pattern or shape than another. The patterns in this book will explain the way each piece should be shaped to achieve the desired end result.

WORKING WITH MORE THAN ONE COLOR

The loop actually on the hook before a stitch is worked forms part of the new stitch. Therefore, if more than one color is being used, you need to change to the new color to complete the last "yarn over hook and draw this loop through" stage. This will avoid messy lines where the 2 colors meet.

FANCY STITCH PATTERNS AND GROUPS

The basic crochet stitches can be grouped together or placed within the work to make a myriad of different effects. Whatever the effect created, each individual stitch will be worked in the way it would be normally—it is how it is placed within the work that creates the stitch pattern.

Sometimes one or more basic stitches are combined to create a special effect or type of stitch. If this is the case, you will find that a special abbreviation is used for this group of stitches, and how this group of stitches should be worked will be explained in the "abbreviations" section of the pattern. Before you start your crochet, it's a good idea to read this section and practice the stitch group so that you know exactly what you are meant to do.

ADDING EDGINGS AND BANDS

Once the main crocheted pieces have been worked and any seams joined, you'll often find that edgings or bands are often worked to complete the item.

To work the edging, start by attaching the yarn at the point the pattern tells you to. Attach the yarn by making a slip knot on the hook and then working a slip stitch at the required position. Complete the edging following the instructions given with the pattern.

Edgings have a tendency to stretch as they are worked—but they are generally needed to hold an edge to a particular length. It's therefore a good idea to work the first round (or row) of any edging a little too tightly. That way, as any further rounds (or rows) are worked, it will gently ease itself out to the correct length.

There are no real hard and fast rules as to exactly how many stitches you need to work along an edge—it's a bit of a trial and error process! If in doubt, work too few stitches—especially if the edging is only one or two rounds (or rows). This can gently be stretched to the right length once you've finished. If, once you've completed your edging, it looks wavy or frilly, pull it out and start again! No matter how many stitches you work, try to space them out evenly along the edge and try not to split the yarn of the existing stitches as you insert the hook into the work.

Crab stitch

This is a version of single crochet and is quite often worked as the last round (or row) of an edging as it creates a neat "beaded" finish that looks virtually the same on both sides.

Almost all crochet stitches are worked from right to left—but crab stitch is different. It is basically just a row of single crochet stitches that are worked the "wrong" way round—from left to right. It can be quite tricky to get the hang of but, once mastered, it gives a really nice finish. To work a crab stitch edging, do NOT turn at the end of the last row (or round)—you are going to be working back along the stitches you've just made. Insert the hook from front to back under the 2 bars

of yarn sitting across the top of next stitch to the right. Take the yarn under the hook and draw this new loop of yarn through the work. Wrap the yarn around the hook in the usual way and draw this new loop through both loops on the hook—exactly as you would for any single crochet stitch. Now insert the hook into the next stitch to the right again, twisting the hook towards you and towards the right as you insert it. Take the yarn under the hook and draw this new loop through the work. Wrap the yarn around the hook again, taking it from the back, over, round and under the hook, and draw this new loop through both loops on the hook. Continue along the edge in this way. As each stitch is made it will form a little knot along the edge of the work. Crab stitch can stretch the edge it's worked along, so make sure the edge is quite "tight" before you start.

CROCHET STITCH DIAGRAMS

Crochet stitch patterns can also be shown as diagrams. These show you exactly how each new set of stitches sits within the work in relation to the previous and next sets of stitches. Each pattern in this book gives you written details of exactly how to work each stitch pattern for each size and piece being made—but you'll also find a diagram that shows the basic stitch pattern. Use this as a visual guide, referring to the written pattern for how many stitches to actually work.

On these stitch diagrams, a different symbol is used for each type of crochet stitch. Below is a list of what these symbols mean.

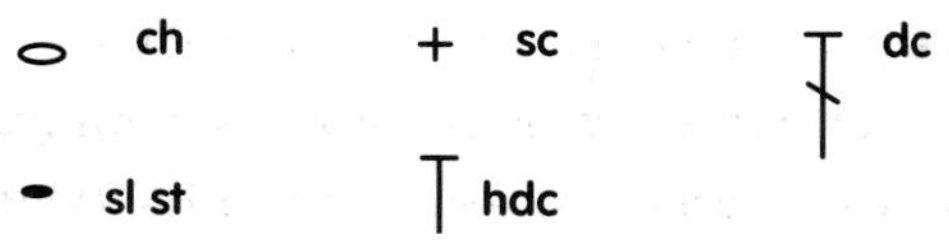

⬯ ch	+ sc	�framentsymbol⟧ dc
• sl st	T hdc	

AFTERCARE

Once your garment is complete, it's a good idea to keep one of the ball bands. This will give you details of exactly how the yarn should be washed. If two yarns are combined within one garment, it should be washed to suit the more delicate yarn. For example, if one yarn is only suitable for hand washing whilst the other can be machine washed, the completed garment must be hand washed.

the patterns

Aran-style jacket

This cozy zip-up jacket features panels of textured diamonds and bobbles, on a base of simple single crochet, which echo traditional aran style knitting—but are surprisingly simple to achieve. Worked in a soft cotton and microfiber mixed yarn, the neat collar completes the look.

MEASUREMENTS

age	0–3	3–6	6–12	12–18	months
chest	16	18	20	22	in
	41	46	51	56	cm
actual chest	18½	20½	22¾	25	in
	47	52	58	64	cm
length	8½	10¼	11¾	13¼	in
	22	26	30	34	cm
sleeve seam	5	6¼	7¾	10¼	in
	13	16	20	26	cm

MATERIALS

• 3 [4:4:5] x 50 g balls of Rowan Calmer in Drift 460
• Sizes D3 (3.00 mm) and E4 (3.50 mm) crochet hooks
• Open-ended zipper to fit

ABBREVIATIONS

• **rbdc**—work dc round stem of next st, inserting hook from right to left and from back to front

• **rfdc**—work dc round stem of next st, inserting hook from right to left and from front to back
• **hdc3tog**—(yo and insert hook as indicated, yo and draw loop through) 3 times, yo and draw through all 7 loops on hook.
See also page 9.

GAUGE

21 stitches and 20 rows to 4 in (10 cm) measured over pattern using a E4 (3.50 mm) hook.
Change hook size if necessary to obtain this gauge.

Pattern panel (16 sts)

1st row (RS): 1 rfdc around stem of next st, 1 sc into each of next 6 sts, skip 1 st, 1 rfdc around stem of next st, 1 rfdc around stem of st just skipped and keeping hook in front of rfdc just worked, 1 sc into each of next 6 sts (there should be the tops of 2 sts skipped between the sets of sc either side of the crossed relief sts), 1 rfdc around stem of next st.

2nd row: 1 rbdc around stem of next st, 1 sc into each of next 5 sts, skip 1 st, (1 rbdc around stem and 1 sc into top) of next st, (1 sc into top and 1 rbdc around stem) of next st, skip 1 st, 1 sc into each of next 5 sts, 1 rbdc around stem of next st.

3rd row: 1 rfdc around stem of next st, 1 sc into each of next 4 sts, skip 1 st, (1 rfdc around stem and 1 sc into top) of next st, 1 sc into each of next 2 sts, skip 1 st, (1 sc into top and 1 rfdc around stem) of next st, 1 sc into each of next 4 sts, 1 rfdc around stem of next st.

4th row: 1 rbdc around stem of next st, 1 sc into each of next 3 sts, skip 1 st, (1 rbdc around stem and 1 sc into top) of next st, 1 sc into each of next 4 sts, (1 sc into top and 1 rbdc around stem) of next st, skip 1 st, 1 sc into each of next 3 sts, 1 rbdc around stem of next st.

5th row: 1 rfdc around stem of next st, 1 sc into each of next 2 sts, skip 1 st, (1 rfdc around stem and 1 sc into top) of

STITCH DIAGRAM

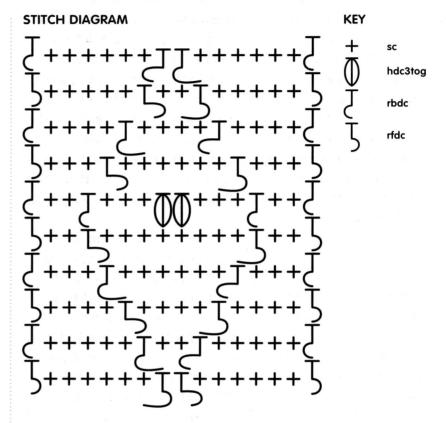

KEY

+ sc

hdc3tog

rbdc

rfdc

next st, 1 sc into each of next 6 sts, skip 1 st, (1 sc into top and 1 rfdc around stem) of next st, 1 sc into each of next 2 sts, 1 rfdc around stem of next st.

6th row: 1 rbdc around stem of next st, 1 sc into each of next 2 sts, 1 rbdc around stem of next st, 1 sc into each of next 3 sts, (hdc3tog into next st) twice, 1 sc into each of next 3 sts, 1 rbdc around stem of next st, 1 sc into each of next 2 sts, 1 rbdc around stem of next st.

7th row: 1 rfdc around stem of next st, 1 sc into each of next 2 sts, (1 sc into

top and 1 rfdc around stem) of next st, skip 1 st, 1 sc into each of next 6 sts, skip 1 st, (1 rfdc around stem and 1 sc into top) of next st, 1 sc into each of next 2 sts, 1 rfdc around stem of next st.

8th row: 1 rbdc around stem of next st, 1 sc into each of next 3 sts, (1 sc into top and 1 rbdc around stem) of next st, skip 1 st, 1 sc into each of next 4 sts, skip 1 st, (1 rbdc around stem and 1 sc into top) of next st, 1 sc into each of next 3 sts, 1 rbdc around stem of next st.

9th row: 1 rfdc around stem of next st,

1 sc into each of next 4 sts, (1 sc into top and 1 rfdc around stem) of next st, skip 1 st, 1 sc into each of next 2 sts, skip 1 st, (1 rfdc around stem and 1 sc into top) of next st, 1 sc into each of next 4 sts, 1 rfdc around stem of next st.

10th row: 1 rbdc around stem of next st, 1 sc into each of next 5 sts, (1 sc into top and 1 rbdc around stem) of next st, skip 2 sts, (1 rbdc around stem and 1 sc into top) of next st, 1 sc into each of next 5 sts, 1 rbdc around stem of next st. These 10 rows form patt panel.

Body

(worked in one piece to armholes)

With D3 (3.00 mm) hook, make 94 [106:118:130] ch.

1st row (RS): 1 sc into 2nd ch from hook, 1 sc into each ch to end, turn. 93 [105:117:129] sts.

2nd row: 1 ch (does NOT count as st), 1 sc into each sc to end, turn.

3rd to 5th rows: As 2nd row.

6th row: 1 ch (does NOT count as st), 1 sc into each of first 4 [6:7:9] sc, *1 hdc into next sc, 1 sc into each of next 6 sc, 2 hdc into next sc, 1 sc into each of next 6 sc, 1 hdc into next sc*, 1 sc into each of next 8 [10:14:16] sc, rep from * to * once more, 1 sc into each of next 9 [13:15:19] sc, rep from * to * once more, 1 sc into each of next 8 [10:14:16] sc, rep from * to * once more, 1 sc into each of last 4 [6:7:9] sc, turn. 97 [109:121:133] sts.

Change to E4 (3.50 mm) hook. Now work in patt as follows:

1st row (RS): 1 ch (does NOT count as st), 1 sc into each of first 4 [6:7:9] sc, work 1st row of patt panel over next 16 sts, 1 sc into each of next 8 [10:14:16] sc, work 1st row of patt panel over next 16 sts, 1 sc into each of next 9 [13:15:19] sc, work 1st row of patt panel over next 16 sts, 1 sc into each of next 8 [10:14:16] sc, work 1st row of patt panel over next 16 sts, 1 sc into each of last 4 [6:7:9] sc, turn.

2nd row: 1 ch (does NOT count as st), 1 sc into each of first 4 [6:7:9] sc, work 2nd row of patt panel over next 16 sts, 1 sc into each of next 8 [10:14:16] sc, work 2nd row of patt panel over next 16 sts, 1 sc into each of next 9 [13:15:19] sc, work 2nd row of patt panel over next 16 sts, 1 sc into each of next 8 [10:14:16] sc, work 2nd row of patt panel over next 16 sts, 1 sc into each of last 4 [6:7:9] sc, turn.

These 2 rows set the sts—4 patt panels with sc fabric between and at sides. Cont as set until Body measures 4 [5:6¼:7½] in (10 [13:16:19] cm).

DIVIDE FOR ARMHOLES

Next row: 1 ch (does NOT count as st), patt 24 [27:30:33] sts and turn, leaving rem sts unworked.

Work on this set of sts only for first front. Cont straight until work measures 3 [3½:3½:4] in (8 [9:9:10] cm), from dividing row, ending at armhole edge.

SHAPE NECK

Next row: 1 ch (does NOT count as st), patt to last 4 [5:5:6] sts and turn, leaving rem sts unworked. 20 [22:25:27] sts. Dec 1 st (by working sc2tog) at neck edge of next 4 rows, then on foll 1 [1:2:2] alt rows. 15 [17:19:21] sts. Cont straight until work measures 4¾ [5:5½:6] in (12 [13:14:15] cm), from dividing row.

SHAPE SHOULDER

Fasten off.

SHAPE BACK

Return to last complete row worked, attach yarn to next sc and cont as follows:

Next row: 1 ch (does NOT count as st), patt 49 [55:61:67] sts and turn, leaving rem sts unworked.

Work on this set of 49 [55:61:67] sts only for back. Cont straight until back matches first front to shoulder.

SHAPE SHOULDER

Fasten off, placing markers either side of center 19 [21:23:25] sts to denote back neck.

SHAPE SECOND FRONT

Return to last complete row worked, attach yarn to next sc and cont as follows:

Next row: 1 ch (does NOT count as st), patt to end, turn. 24 [27:30:33] sts. Complete to match first front, reversing shapings.

Sleeves

With D3 (3.00 mm) hook, make 27 [29:31:33] ch and join with a sl st to form a ring.

1st round (RS): 1 ch (does NOT count as st), 1 sc into each ch to end, sl st to first sc, turn. 27 [29:31:33] sts.

2nd round: 1 ch (does NOT count as st), 1 sc into each sc to end, sl st to first sc, turn.

3rd to 5th rounds: As 2nd round.

6th round: 1 ch (does NOT count as st), 1 sc into each of first 6 [7:8:9] sc, 1 hdc into next sc, 1 sc into each of next 6 sc, 2 hdc into next sc, 1 sc into each of next 6 sc, 1 hdc into next sc, 1 sc into each of last 6 [7:8:9] sc, sl st to first sc, turn. 28 [30:32:34] sts.

Change to E4 (3.50 mm) hook.

Now work in patt as follows:

1st round (RS): 1 ch (does NOT count as st), 2 sc into first sc, 1 sc into each of next 5 [6:7:8] sc, work 1st row of patt panel over next 16 sts, 1 sc into each of next 5 [6:7:8] sc, 2 sc into last sc, sl st to first sc, turn. 30 [32:34:36] sts.

2nd round: 1 ch (does NOT count as st), 2 [1:1:1] sc into first sc, 1 sc into each of next 6 [7:8:9] sc, work 2nd row of patt panel over next 16 sts, 1 sc into each of next 6 [7:8:9] sc, 2 [1:1:1] sc into last sc, sl st to first sc, turn. 32 [32:34:36] sts.

These 2 rounds set the sts—central patt panel with sc fabric at sides.

Cont as set, inc 1 st (by working twice

into first and last sc) at each end of next [next:next:2nd] and 8 [9:6:10] foll alt [alt:alt:3rd] rounds, then at each end of 0 [1:5:2] foll 0 [3rd:3rd:4th] rounds. 50 [54:58:62] sts.
Cont straight until Sleeve measures 5 [6¼:7¾:10¼] in (13 [16:20:26] cm). Fasten off.

Finishing

Join shoulder seams. Insert sleeves into armholes, matching center of last row to shoulder seam and top of "sleeve seam" to underarm.

LEFT FRONT EDGING

With RS facing and using D3 (3.00 mm) hook, rejoin yarn at start of left front neck shaping, 1 ch (does NOT count as st), work 1 row of sc evenly down entire left front opening edge.
Fasten off.

RIGHT FRONT EDGING

With RS facing and using D3 (3.00 mm) hook, rejoin yarn at base of right front opening edge, 1 ch (does NOT count as st), work 1 row of sc evenly up entire right front opening edge to neck shaping.
Do NOT fasten off.

COLLAR

With RS facing, using D3 (3.00 mm) hook and yarn on hook from Right Front Edging, work 1 row of sc evenly around entire neck edge, ending at top of Left Front Edging and ensure number of sc worked is an odd number, turn.
Next row: 1 ch (does NOT count as st), 1 sc into first sc, *2 sc into next sc, 1 sc into next sc, rep from * to end, turn.
Next row: 1 ch (does NOT count as st), 1 sc into each sc to end, turn.
Rep last row until Collar measures 2¼ [2¼:2¾:2¾] in (6 [6:7:7] cm). Fasten off.

Insert zipper into front opening.

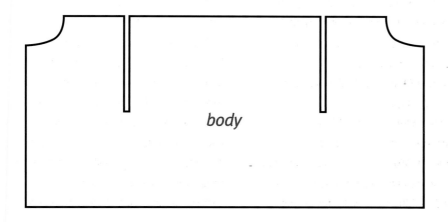

body

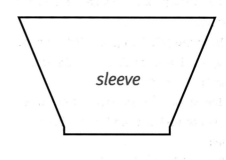

sleeve

Frill-trimmed cardigan

Simple stripes of doubles in a classic yarn and single crochet in a fluffy yarn make up this pretty cardigan. Use two shades of red to create textured stripes, as here, or choose contrasting colors for a bolder look. The fluffy frill edging finishes off the feminine feel!

MEASUREMENTS

age	0–3	3–6	6–12	12–18	months
chest	16	18	20	22	in
	41	46	51	56	cm
actual chest	18	20	22	24	in
	46	51	56	61	cm
full length	9	10½	12	13¼	in
	23	27	31	34	cm
sleeve seam	5	6¼	7½	8¼	in
	13	16	19	21	cm

MATERIALS

- 2 [2:3:3] x 50 g balls of Rowan RYC Cashsoft DK in A (512)
- 3 [3:3:4] x 25 g balls of Rowan Kidsilk Aura in B (760)
- Size G6 (4.00 mm) crochet hook

ABBREVIATIONS

See page 9.

GAUGE

16 stitches and 11½ rows to 4 in (10 cm) measured over pattern using a G6 (4.00 mm) hook.
Change hook size if necessary to obtain this gauge.

STITCH DIAGRAM

KEY

○	ch
+	sc
┃	dc

Shaping note

Decreases

Work all decreases at beg and ends of
rows by working 2 sts together. On 1st
and 4th patt rows, work dec at beg of
row by working "3 ch (does NOT count as
st—remember NOT to work into top of
this 3 ch when working next row!), 1 dc
into next st—1 st decreased" and work
dec at end of row by working "dc2tog
over last 2 sts." On 2nd and 3rd patt
rows, work dec at beg of row by working
"1 ch (does NOT count as st), sc2tog over
first 2 sts—1 st decreased" and work dec
at end of row by working "sc2tog over
last 2 sts."

At top of sleeve, dec 2 sts at each end
of row by working "1 sl st into each of first
3 sts, make turning ch as required, patt
to last 2 sts and turn, leaving rem 2 sts
unworked."

Increases

Work all increases at beg and ends of
rows by working 2 sts into one st of
previous row. On 1st and 4th patt rows,
work inc at beg of row by working "3 ch
(counts as first dc), 1 dc into st at base of
3 ch—1 st increased" and work inc at
end of row by working "2 dc into last st."
On 2nd and 3rd patt rows, work inc at
beg of row by working "1 ch (does NOT
count as st), 2 sc into first st—1 st
increased" and work inc at end of row
by working "2 sc into last st."

Body

(worked in one piece to armholes)

With G6 (4.00 mm hook and A, make
77 [85:93:101] ch.

Foundation row (RS): 1 dc into 4th ch from
hook, 1 dc into each ch to end, turn.
75 [83:91:99] sts.

Now work in patt as follows:

1st row (WS): Using A, 3 ch (counts as first
dc), skip dc at base of 3 ch, 1 dc into each
dc to end, working last dc into top of 3 ch
at beg of previous row, turn.

Join in B.

2nd row: Using B, 1 ch (does NOT count as
st), 1 sc into each dc to end, working last sc
into top of 3 ch at beg of previous row,
turn.

3rd row: Using B, 1 ch (does NOT count as
st), 1 sc into each sc to end, turn.

4th row: Using A, 3 ch (counts as first dc),
skip sc at base of 3 ch, 1 dc into each sc to
end, turn.

These 4 rows form patt.

Cont in patt for a further 8 [11:14:17] rows,
ending after 1 [2:1:2] rows using A [B:B:A].
(Body should measure approx 4¼
[5½:6½:7½] in, 11 [14:17:19] cm.)

DIVIDE FOR ARMHOLES

Keeping patt and stripes correct, cont as
follows:

Next row: Patt 17 [19:21:23] sts and turn,
leaving rem sts unworked.

Work on this set of 17 [19:21:23] sts only for
first front.

Dec 1 st at each end of next 4 rows.
9 [11:13:15] sts.

Dec 1 st at front slope edge only of next
2 [3:4:5] rows, then on foll 2 alt rows.
5 [6:7:8] sts.

Work 1 row, ending after 1 row using yarn
A. (Armhole should measure
4 [4¼:4¾:5] in,10 [11:12:13] cm.)

SHAPE SHOULDER

Fasten off.

SHAPE BACK

Return to last complete row worked, skip
next 4 sts, attach yarn to next st and cont
as follows:

Next row: Patt 33 [37:41:45] sts and turn,
leaving rem sts unworked.

Work on this set of 33 [37:41:45] sts only
for back.

Dec 1 st at each end of next 4 rows.
25 [29:33:37] sts.

Work 7 [8:9:10] rows, ending after 1 row
using yarn A.

SHAPE SHOULDER

Fasten off, placing markers either side of
center 15 [17:19:21] sts to denote back neck.

SHAPE SECOND FRONT

Return to last complete row worked, skip
next 4 sts, attach yarn to next st and cont
as follows:

Next row: Patt to end, turn.
17 [19:21:23] sts.

Complete to match first front, reversing
shapings.

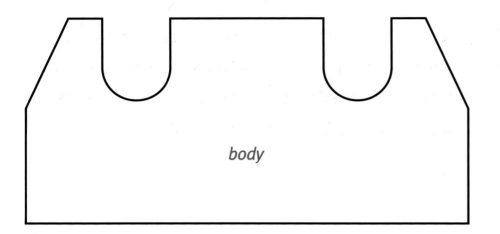

body

sleeve

Sleeves

With a size G6 (4.00 mm) hook and A, make 21 [23:25:27] ch.

Work foundation row as given for Body. 19 [21:23:25] sts.

Starting with 1st patt row, cont in patt as given for Body, inc 1 st at each end of next and foll 5 [6:3:3] alt rows, then on 0 [0:3:4] foll 3rd rows. 31 [35:37:41] sts.

Work 1 [2:2:2] rows, ending after 1 [2:1:2] rows using A [B:B:A]. (Sleeve should measure approx 4¼ [5½:6½:7½] in, 11 [14:17:19] cm.)

SHAPE TOP

Keeping patt and stripes correct, dec 2 sts at each end of next row. 27 [31:33:37] sts.

Dec 1 st at each end of next 6 [7:8:9] rows, ending after 2 rows using B.
15 [17:17:19] sts.

Fasten off.

Finishing

Join shoulder seams.

HEM FRILL

With RS facing, using G6 (4.00 mm) hook and B, rejoin yarn at base of left front opening edge, 1 ch (does NOT count as st), work 1 row of sc evenly across entire foundation ch edge of Body, turn.

Next row: 4 ch (counts as first dc and 1 ch), skip sc at base of 4 ch, 1 dc into next sc, *1 ch, 1 dc into next sc, rep from * to end, turn.

Next row: 4 ch (counts as first dc and 1 ch), skip dc at base of 4 ch, *1 dc into next ch sp, 1 ch**, 1 dc into next dc, 1 ch, rep from * to end, ending last rep at **, 1 dc into 3rd of 4 ch at beg of previous row. Fasten off.

CUFF FRILLS (BOTH ALIKE)

Work as given for Hem frill.

Join sleeve and cuff frill seams. Insert sleeves into armholes, matching center of last row to shoulder seam and top of sleeve seam to center of sts skipped at underarm.

FRONT AND NECK FRILL

With RS facing, using G6 (4.00 mm) hook and B, rejoin yarn at base of right front opening edge (this is top of last row of Hem frill), 1 ch (does NOT count as st), work 1 row of sc evenly up entire right front opening and neck edge, across back neck, then down entire left from slope and opening edge, turn.
Complete as given for Hem and Cuff frills.

TIES (MAKE 2)

With G6 (4.00 mm) hook and A, make a ch approx 9¾ in (25 cm) long.

Next row: 1 sc into 2nd ch from hook, 1 sc into each ch to end.
Fasten off.

Attach Ties to inside of first row of Front and Neck Frill, level with start of front slope shaping.

Cozy cardigan

A classic cardigan for all seasons given a new twist with a versatile textured stitch! The simple two-row pattern uses just basic stitches to create the boxed bobble effect—and it will look just as good on a baby boy or baby girl!

MEASUREMENTS

age	0–3	3–6	6–12	12–18	months
chest	16	18	20	22	in
	41	46	51	56	cm
actual chest	18½	21¼	24	26¾	in
	47	54	61	68	cm
length	9	9¾	11	13¼	in
	23	25	28	34	cm
sleeve seam	5	6¼	7¾	9¾	in
	13	16	20	25	cm

MATERIALS

• 3 [3:4:4] x 50 g balls of Rowan Pure Wool DK in Pier 006
• Sizes E4 (3.50 mm) and G6 (4.00 mm) crochet hooks
• 5 buttons

ABBREVIATIONS

• hdc3tog—(yo and insert hook as indicated, yo and draw loop through) 3 times, yo and draw through all 7 loops on hook.
See also page 9.

GAUGE

17 stitches and 11 rows to 4 in (10 cm) measured over pattern using G6 (4.00 mm) hook.
Change hook size if necessary to obtain this gauge.

SHAPING NOTE

When working shaping through patt, work part patt reps as hdc fabric (by working 1 hdc into each st).

STITCH DIAGRAM

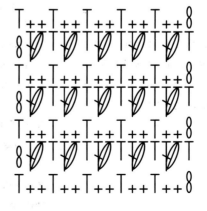

KEY

○ ch
+ sc
T hdc
T dc

Body

(worked in one piece to armholes)

With E4 (3.50 mm) hook, make 77 [89:101:113] ch.

1st row (WS): 1 sc into 2nd ch from hook, 1 sc into each ch to end, turn. 76 [88:100:112] sts.

2nd row: 1 ch (does NOT count as st), 1 sc into each sc to end, turn.

3rd to 5th rows: As 2nd row.

Change to G6 (4.00 mm) hook.

6th row: 2 ch (counts as first hdc), skip sc at base of 2 ch, *1 sc into each of next 2 sc, 1 hdc into next sc, rep from * to end, turn.

Now work in patt as follows:

1st row (WS): 2 ch (counts as first hdc), skip hdc at base of 2 ch, *1 dc into next sc, hdc3tog around stem of dc just worked, skip 1 sc, 1 hdc into next hdc, rep from * to end, working hdc at end of last rep into top of 2 ch at beg of previous row, turn. 25 [29:33:37] patt reps.

2nd row: 2 ch (counts as first hdc), skip hdc at base of 2 ch, *1 sc into next hdc3tog, 1 sc into next dc, 1 hdc into next hdc, rep from * to end, working hdc at end of last rep into top of 2 ch at beg of previous row, turn.

These 2 rows form patt.

Cont in patt until Body measures approx 4¾ [5½:6:8¼] in (12 [14:15:21] cm), ending with RS facing for next row.

DIVIDE FOR ARMHOLES

Next row: 2 ch (counts as first hdc), skip hdc at base of 2 ch, [1 sc into next hdc3tog, 1 sc into next dc, 1 hdc into next hdc] 5 [6:7:8] times and turn, leaving rem sts unworked.

Work on this set of 16 [19:22:25] sts only for right front.

Work 7 rows, ending with RS facing for next row.

SHAPE NECK

Next row: Sl st across and into 5th [8th:6th:6th] st—4 [7:5:5] sts dec, 2 ch (counts as first hdc), skip st at base of 2 ch, patt to end, turn. 12 [12:17:20] sts.

Next row: Patt 11 [11:16:19] sts and turn, leaving rem st unworked—1 st dec.

Next row: Sl st across and into 2nd st—1 st dec, 2 ch (counts as first hdc), skip st at base of 2 ch, patt to end, turn. 10 [10:15:18] sts.

3rd and 4th sizes only

Next row: Patt [14:17] sts and turn, leaving rem sts unworked—1 st dec.

Next row: Sl st across and into 2nd st—1 st decreased, 2 ch (counts as first hdc), skip st at base of 2 ch, patt to end, turn. [13:16] sts.

All sizes

Work 2 rows, ending with WS facing for next row.

SHAPE SHOULDER

Fasten off.

SHAPE BACK

Return to last complete row worked, skip next 5 sts, attach yarn to next st and cont as follows:

Next row: 2 ch (counts as first hdc), skip st at base of 2 ch, patt 33 [39:45:51] sts and turn, leaving rem sts unworked.

Work on this set of 34 [40:46:52] sts only for back.

Work 12 [12:14:14] rows, ending with WS facing for next row.

SHAPE SHOULDER

Fasten off, placing markers either side of center 14 [20:20:20] sts to denote back neck.

SHAPE LEFT FRONT

Return to last complete row worked, skip next 5 sts, attach yarn to next st and cont as follows:

Next row: 2 ch (counts as first hdc), skip st at base of 2 ch, patt to end, turn. 16 [19:22:25] sts.

Complete to match right front, reversing shapings.

Sleeves

With E4 (3.50 mm) hook, make 23 [26:26:29] ch.

1st row (WS): 1 sc into 2nd ch from hook, 1 sc into each ch to end, turn. 22 [25:25:28] sts.

2nd row: 1 ch (does NOT count as st), 1 sc into each sc to end, turn.

3rd to 5th rows: As 2nd row.

Change to G6 (4.00 mm) hook.

6th row: 2 ch (counts as first hdc), skip sc

at base of 2 ch, *1 sc into each of next 2 sc, 1 hdc into next sc, rep from * to end, turn. Now work in patt as follows:

1st row (WS): 2 ch (counts as first hdc), 1 hdc into hdc at base of 2 ch—1 st increased, *1 dc into next sc, hdc3tog around stem of dc just worked, skip 1 sc**, 1 hdc into next hdc, rep from * to end, ending last rep at **, 2 hdc into top of 2 ch at beg of previous row—1 st increased, turn. 24 [27:27:30] sts.

Working all increases as set by last row and working inc sts in hdc fabric until there are sufficient to work in patt, cont as follows:

Work 0 [1:1:2] rows.

Inc 1 st at each end of next 4 [1:1:1] rows, then on foll 2 [3:7:0] alt rows, then on 0 [1:0:6] foll 3rd rows. 36 [37:43:44] sts.

Work 1 [2:1:2] rows, ending with WS facing for next row.

SHAPE TOP

Place markers at both ends of last row to denote top of sleeve seam.

Work a further 2 rows.

Fasten off.

Finishing

Join shoulder seams. Join sleeve seams. Insert sleeves into armholes, matching center of last row to shoulder seam and top of sleeve seam to center of sts skipped at underarm.

NECKBAND

With RS facing and using E4 (3.50 mm) hook, rejoin yarn at top of right front opening edge, 1 ch (does NOT count as st), work 1 row of sc evenly around entire neck edge, ending at top of left front opening edge, turn.

Next row: 1 ch (does NOT count as st), 1 sc into each sc to end, working sc2tog as required to ensure Neckband lays flat, turn.

Rep last row 3 times more.

Fasten off.

BUTTON BAND

With RS facing and using E4 (3.50 mm) hook, rejoin yarn at top of left end of Neckband for a girl, or base of right front opening edge for a boy, 1 ch (does NOT count as st), work 1 row of sc evenly along entire front opening edge, between top of Neckband and foundation ch edge.

1st row: 1 ch (does NOT count as st), 1 sc into each sc to end, turn.

Rep last row 3 times more.

Fasten off.

Mark positions for 5 buttons on this Band—first to come ½ in (12 mm) up from lower edge, last to come ½ in (12 mm) down from top of Neckband, and rem 3 buttons evenly spaced between.

BUTTONHOLE BAND

Work to match Button Band, making buttonholes in 3rd row to correspond with positions marked for buttons by replacing "1 sc into each of next 2 sc" with "2 ch, skip 2 sc." (On foll row, work 2 sc into this buttonhole ch sp.)

Sew on buttons.

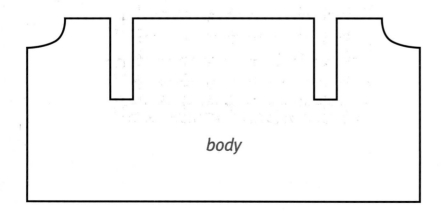

body

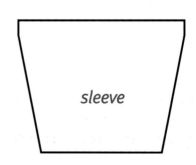

sleeve

Duffle coat

Made in a really chunky pure wool yarn, using just single crochet, you will have this cozy coat made in no time. And its clever construction means there are virtually no seams to sew up afterwards—making it even easier to complete!

MEASUREMENTS

age	0–3	3–6	6–12	12–18	months
chest	16	18	20	22	in
	41	46	51	56	cm
actual chest	18	21¼	23½	26¼	in
	46	54	60	67	cm
length	11	13¼	15¾	17¼	in
	28	34	40	44	cm
sleeve seam	4¾	6	7¾	9	in
	12	15	20	23	cm

MATERIALS

• 4 [5:5:6] x 100 g balls of Rowan Big Wool in Whoosh 014
• 7.00 mm hook
• 3 buttons

ABBREVIATIONS

See page 9.

GAUGE

9 stitches and 10 rows to 4 in (10 cm) measured over pattern using 7.00 mm hook.

Change hook size if necessary to obtain this gauge.

STITCH DIAGRAM

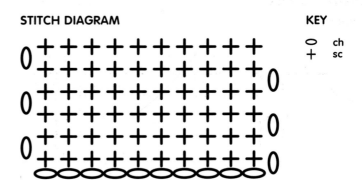

KEY

O ch
+ sc

Body

(worked in one piece to armholes)

With 7.00 mm hook, make 61 [72:81:92] ch.

1st row (RS): 1 sc into 2nd ch from hook, 1 sc into each ch to end, turn. 60 [71:80:91] sts.

2nd row: 1 ch (does NOT count as st), 1 sc into each st to end, turn.

This row forms patt.

Work 2 rows.

5th row: 1 ch (does NOT count as st), 1 sc into each of first 8 [9:9:10] sc, sc2tog over next 2 sc, (1 sc into each of next 12 [15:18:21] sc, sc2tog over next 2 sc) 3 times, 1 sc into each of last 8 [9:9:10] sc, turn. 56 [67:76:87] sts.

Work 3 rows.

9th row: 1 ch (does NOT count as st), 1 sc into each of first 6 [7:7:11] sc, sc2tog over next 2 sc, (1 sc into each of next 12 [15:18:19] sc, sc2tog over next 2 sc) 3 times, 1 sc into each of last 6 [7:7:11] sc, turn. 52 [63:72:83] sts. Work 3 rows.

13th row: 1 ch (does NOT count as st), 1 sc into each of first 7 [8:8:9] sc, sc2tog over next 2 sc, (1 sc into each of next 10 [13:16:19] sc, sc2tog over next 2 sc) 3 times, 1 sc into each of last 7 [8:8:9] sc, turn. 48 [59:68:79] sts.

2nd, 3rd and 4th sizes only

Work 3 rows.

17th row: 1 ch (does NOT count as st), 1 sc into each of first [6:6:10] sc, sc2tog over next 2 sc, (1 sc into each of next [13:16:17] sc, sc2tog over next 2 sc) 3 times, 1 sc into each of last [6:6:10] sc, turn. [55:64:75] sts.

3rd and 4th sizes only

Work 3 rows.

21st row: 1 ch (does NOT count as st), 1 sc into each of first [7:8] sc, sc2tog over next 2 sc, (1 sc into each of next [14:17] sc, sc2tog over next 2 sc) 3 times, 1 sc into each of last [7:8] sc, turn. [60:71] sts.

4th size only

Work 3 rows.

25th row: 1 ch (does NOT count as st), 1 sc into each of first 9 sc, sc2tog over next 2 sc, (1 sc into each of next 15 sc, sc2tog over next 2 sc) 3 times, 1 sc into each of last 9 sc, turn. 67 sts.

All sizes

Work 3 [4:5:4] rows on rem 48 [55:60:67] sts, ending with RS [WS:RS:WS] facing for next row.

Break yarn.

Sleeves

With 7.00 mm hook, make 12 [13:14:15] ch and join with a sl st to form a ring.

1st round (RS): 1 ch (does NOT count as st), 1 sc into each ch to end, sl st to first sc, turn. 12 [13:14:15] sts.

Note: You must turn at the end of every round so that the sleeve fabric matches the body fabric.

2nd round: 1 ch (does NOT count as st), 1 sc into each sc to end, sl st to first sc, turn. This round forms patt.

3rd round: 1 ch (does NOT count as st), 2 sc into first sc—1 st increased, 1 sc into each sc to last sc, 2 sc into last sc—1 st increased, sl st to first sc, turn. 14 [15:16:17] sts.

Working all increases as set by last round, inc 1 st at each end of 2nd [2nd:3rd:3rd] and foll 3 [1:0:0] alt rounds, then on 0 [2:4:2] foll 3rd rounds, then on 0 [0:0:2] foll 4th rounds. 22 [23:26:27] sts.

Work 1 [2:2:3] rounds, ending with RS [WS:RS:WS] facing for next round.

Break yarn.

Yoke

With RS [WS:RS:WS] facing and 7.00 mm hook, rejoin yarn to last st of last row of Body and join Body and Sleeves as follows:

1st row: 1 ch (does NOT count as st), 1 sc into each of first 11 [13:14:16] sc of Body, skip first 2 sc of next round of first Sleeve, 1 sc into each of next 18 [19:22:23] sc of Sleeve, skip last 2 sc of Sleeve and next 4 sc of Body, 1 sc into each of next 18 [21:24:27] sc of Body, skip first 2 sc of next round of second Sleeve, 1 sc into each of next 18 [19:22:23] sc of Sleeve, skip last 2 sc of Sleeve and next 4 sc of Body, 1 sc into each of last 11 [13:14:16] sc of Body, turn. 76 [85:96:105] sts.

2nd row: 1 ch (does NOT count as st), 1 sc into each of first 11 [13:14:14] sc, *(sc2tog over next 2 sc) 1 [1:1:2] times, 1 sc into each of next 14 [15:18:19] sc, (sc2tog over next 2 sc) 1 [1:1:2] times*, 1 sc into each of next 18 [21:24:23] sc, rep from * to * once more, 1 sc into each of last 11 [13:14:14] sc, turn. 72 [81:92:97] sts.

3rd row: 1 ch (does NOT count as st), 1 sc into each of first 11 [13:12:15] sc, *(sc2tog over

next 2 sc) 1 [1:2:1] times, 1 sc into each of next 12 [13:16:17] sc, (sc2tog over next 2 sc) 1 [1:2:1] times*, 1 sc into each of next 18 [21:20:25] sc, rep from * to * once more, 1 sc into each of last 11 [13:12:15] sc, turn. 68 [77:84:93] sts.

4th row: 1 ch (does NOT count as st), 1 sc into each of first 9 [11:13:13] sc, *(sc2tog over next 2 sc) 2 [2:1:2] times, 1 sc into each of next 10 [11:14:15] sc, (sc2tog over next 2 sc) 2 [2:1:2] times*, 1 sc into each of next 14 [17:22:21] sc, rep from * to * once more, 1 sc into each of last 9 [11:13:13] sc, turn. 60 [69:80:85] sts.

5th row: 1 ch (does NOT count as st), 1 sc into each of first 10 [12:11:14] sc, *(sc2tog over next 2 sc) 1 [1:2:1] times, 1 sc into each of next 8 [9:12:13] sc, (sc2tog over next 2 sc) 1 [1:2:1] times*, 1 sc into each of next 16 [19:18:23] sc, rep from * to * once more, 1 sc into each of last 10 [12:11:14] sc, turn. 56 [65:72:81] sts.

6th row: 1 ch (does NOT count as st), 1 sc into each of first 10 [10:12:12] sc, *(sc2tog over next 2 sc) 1 [2:1:2] times, 1 sc into each of next 6 [7:10:11] sc, (sc2tog over next 2 sc) 1 [2:1:2] times*, 1 sc into each of next 16 [15:20:19] sc, rep from * to * once more, 1 sc into each of last 10 [10:12:12] sc, turn. 52 [57:68:73] sts.

7th row: 1 ch (does NOT count as st), 1 sc into each of first 8 [11:10:13] sc, *(sc2tog over next 2 sc) 2 [0:2:0] times, 1 sc into each of next 4 [9:8:13] sc, (sc2tog over next 2 sc) 2 [0:2:0] times*, 1 sc into each of next 12 [17:16:21] sc, rep from * to * once more, 1 sc into each of last 8 [11:10:13] sc, turn.

44 [57:60:73] sts.

8th row: 1 ch (does NOT count as st), 1 sc into each of first 9 [9:11:11] sc, *(sc2tog over next 2 sc) 0 [2:0:2] times, 1 sc into each of next 6 [5:10:9] sc, (sc2tog over next 2 sc) 0 [2:0:2] times*, 1 sc into each of next 14 [13:18:17] sc, rep from * to * once more, 1 sc into each of last 9 [9:11:11] sc, turn. 44 [49:60:65] sts.

9th row: 1 ch (does NOT count as st), 1 sc into each of first 7 [10:9:12] sc, *(sc2tog over next 2 sc) 2 [0:2:0] times, 1 sc into each of next 2 [7:6:11] sc, (sc2tog over next 2 sc) 2 [0:2:0] times*, 1 sc into each of next 10 [15:14:19] sc, rep from * to * once more, 1 sc into each of last 7 [10:9:12] sc, turn. 36 [49:52:65] sts.

10th row: 1 ch (does NOT count as st), 1 sc into each of first 8 [8:10:10] sc, *(sc2tog over next 2 sc) 0 [2:0:2] times, 1 sc into each of next 4 [3:8:7] sc, (sc2tog over next 2 sc) 0 [2:0:2] times*, 1 sc into each of next 12 [11:16:15] sc, rep from * to * once more, 1 sc into each of last 8 [8:10:10] sc, turn. 36 [41:52:57] sts.

11th row: 1 ch (does NOT count as st), 1 sc into each of first 6 [9:8:11] sc, *(sc2tog over next 2 sc) 2 [0:2:0] times, 1 sc into each of next 0 [5:4:9] sc, (sc2tog over next 2 sc) 2 [0:2:0] times*, 1 sc into each of next 8 [13:12:17] sc, rep from * to * once more, 1 sc into each of last 6 [9:8:11] sc, turn. 28 [41:44:57] sts.

2nd, 3rd and 4th sizes only

12th row: 1 ch (does NOT count as st), 1 sc into each of first [7:9:9] sc, *(sc2tog over next

2 sc) [2:0:2] times, 1 sc into each of next [1:6:5] sc, (sc2tog over next 2 sc) [2:0:2] times*, 1 sc into each of next [9:14:13] sc, rep from * to * once more, 1 sc into each of last [7:9:9] sc, turn. [33:44:49] sts.

3rd and 4th sizes only

13th row: 1 ch (does NOT count as st), 1 sc into each of first [7:10] sc, *(sc2tog over next 2 sc) [2:0] times, 1 sc into each of next [2:7] sc, (sc2tog over next 2 sc) [2:0] times*, 1 sc into each of next [10:15] sc, rep from * to * once more, 1 sc into each of last [7:10] sc, turn. [36:49] sts.

4th size only

14th row: 1 ch (does NOT count as st), 1 sc into each of first 8 sc, *(sc2tog over next 2 sc) twice, 1 sc into each of next 3 sc, (sc2tog over next 2 sc) twice*, 1 sc into each of next 11 sc, rep from * to * once more, 1 sc into each of last 8 sc, turn. 41 sts.

All sizes

Next row (WS): 1 ch (does NOT count as st), 1 sc into each sc to end, turn. 28 [33:36:41] sts.

SHAPE FOR HOOD

Next row: 1 ch (does NOT count as st), 1 sc into each of first 3 [2:3:2] sc, (sc2tog over next 2 sc, 1 sc into each of next 2 sc) 5 [3:7:4] times, (sc2tog over next 2 sc, 1 sc into next sc) 0 [1:0:1] times, (sc2tog over next 2 sc, 1 sc into each of next 2 sc) 0 [3:0:4] times, sc2tog over next 2 sc, 1 sc into each of last 3 [2:3:2] sc, turn. 22 [25:28:31] sts. Work 1 row.

Next row: 1 ch (does NOT count as st), 1 sc into each of first 7 [9:11:13] sc, 2 sc into each of next 8 [7:6:5] sc, 1 sc into each of last 7 [9:11:13] sc, turn. 30 [32:34:36] sts. Work 14 [15:16:17] rows.

Next row: 1 ch (does NOT count as st), 1 sc into each of first 13 [14:15:16] sc, (sc2tog over next 2 sc) twice, 1 sc into each of last 13 [14:15:16] sc, turn. 28 [30:32:34] sts. Work 1 row.

Next row: 1 ch (does NOT count as st), 1 sc into each of first 12 [13:14:15] sc, (sc2tog over next 2 sc) twice, 1 sc into each of last 12 [13:14:15] sc, turn. 26 [28:30:32] sts.

Next row: 1 ch (does NOT count as st), 1 sc into each of first 11 [12:13:14] sc, (sc2tog over next 2 sc) twice, 1 sc into each of last 11 [12:13:14] sc, turn. 24 [26:28:30] sts. Fold Hood in half with RS together and join top of Hood by working 1 row of sc through both layers.
Fasten off.

Finishing

Join underarm seams. Sew on buttons, placing buttons on 3rd st in from front opening edge (on left front for a girl, or right front for a boy), positioning lowest button 3 [4:4¾:5½] in (8 [10:12:14] cm) up from lower edge, top button 2¼ [2¼:2¾:2¾] in (6 [6:7:7] cm) down from first row of Hood and rem button evenly spaced between. Push buttons through fabric of other front to fasten.

Blanket

The fully reversible stitch used for this blanket means it will look just as good whichever way baby snuggles up. And the soft, machine-washable cotton and microfiber yarn makes it practical too. Choose a dramatic shade, as here, or a pretty pastel color—either way it is bound to keep baby cozy.

MEASUREMENTS

Finished size   27½ x 35½ in
                         70 x 90 cm

MATERIALS

• 14 x 50 g balls of Rowan All Seasons Cotton in Jazz 185
• Size H8 (5.00 mm) crochet hook

ABBREVIATIONS

• hdc3tog—(yo and insert hook as indicated, yo and draw loop through) 3 times, yo and draw through all 7 loops on hook.
See also page 9

GAUGE

15 stitches and 9 rows to 4 in (10 cm) measured over pattern using H8 (5.00 mm) hook.
Change hook size if necessary to obtain this gauge.

STITCH DIAGRAM

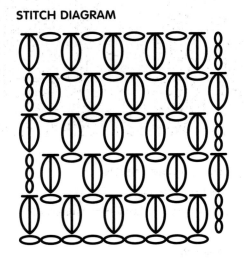

KEY

  ch

hdc3tog

Blanket

With H8 (5.00 mm) hook, make 102 ch.

1st row (RS): 1 hdc3tog into 4th ch from hook, *1 ch, skip 1 ch, 1 hdc3tog into next ch, rep from * to end, turn. 100 sts.

2nd row: 3 ch (counts as first st), skip hdc3tog at base of 3 ch, 1 hdc3tog into next ch sp, *1 ch, skip 1 hdc3tog, 1 hdc3tog into next ch sp, rep from * to end, working last hdc3tog between hdc3tog and 3 ch at beg of previous row, turn.

This row forms patt.

Cont in patt until Blanket measures 34¼ in (87 cm).

Fasten off.

Finishing

BORDER

With RS facing and using H8 (5.00 mm) hook, rejoin yarn to outer edge of Blanket, 1 ch (does NOT count as st), work 1 round of sc evenly around entire outer edge, working 3 sc into each corner point and ending with sl st to first sc, turn.

Next round: 1 ch (does NOT count as st), 1 sc into each sc to end, working 3 sc into each corner point and ending with sl st to first sc.

Fasten off.

Hat, booties, and mittens

This classic hat, mittens and booties set is given a modern look, made in a clever multicolored and hand-dyed yarn. Worked in rounds of simple single crochet, the set is really easy to make and there are almost no seams to sew up afterwards.

MEASUREMENTS

age	0–3	3–6	6–12	12–18	months
HAT					
width around head	13¼	14½	15¾	17	in
	34	37	40	43	cm
BOOTIES					
length of foot	4	4¼	4¾	5	in
	10	11	12	13	cm
MITTENS					
width around hand	3½	4	4¼	4¾	in
	9	10	11	12	cm

MATERIALS
• 1 [2:2:2] x 110 g hanks of Colinette Jitterbug in Mardi Gras 155
• Size C2 (2.50 mm) crochet hook

ABBREVIATIONS
See page 9.

GAUGE
21 stitches and 26 rows to 4 in (10 cm) measured over sc fabric using C2 (2.50 mm) hook. Change hook size if necessary to obtain this gauge.

STITCH DIAGRAM

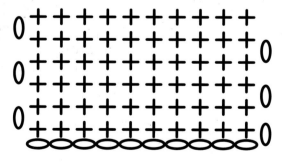

KEY
○ ch
+ sc

Hat

With C2 (2.50 mm) hook, make 72 [78:84:90] ch and join with a sl st to form a ring.

1st round (RS): 1 ch (does NOT count as st), 1 sc into each ch to end, sl st to first sc, turn. 72 [78:84:90] sts.

2nd round: 1 ch (does NOT count as st), 1 sc into each sc to end, sl st to first sc, turn. This round forms sc fabric.

Cont in sc fabric until Hat measures 5 in (13 cm), ending with RS facing for next round.

4th size only

Next round (RS): 1 ch (does NOT count as st), (1 sc into each of next 13 sc, sc2tog over next 2 sc) 6 times, sl st to first sc, turn. 84 sts. Work 1 round, ending with RS facing for next round.

3rd and 4th sizes only

Next round (RS): 1 ch (does NOT count as st), (1 sc into each of next 12 sc, sc2tog over next 2 sc) 6 times, sl st to first sc, turn. 78 sts. Work 1 round, ending with RS facing for next round.

2nd, 3rd and 4th sizes only

Next round (RS): 1 ch (does NOT count as st), (1 sc into each of next 11 sc, sc2tog over next 2 sc) 6 times, sl st to first sc, turn. 72 sts. Work 1 round, ending with RS facing for next round.

All sizes

Next round (RS): 1 ch (does NOT count as st), (1 sc into each of next 10 sc, sc2tog over next 2 sc) 6 times, sl st to first sc, turn. 66 sts. Work 1 round.

Next round: 1 ch (does NOT count as st), (1 sc into each of next 9 sc, sc2tog over next 2 sc) 6 times, sl st to first sc, turn. 60 sts.

Next round: 1 ch (does NOT count as st), (sc2tog over next 2 sc, 1 sc into each of next 8 sc) 6 times, sl st to first sc, turn. 54 sts.

Next round: 1 ch (does NOT count as st), (1 sc into each of next 7 sc, sc2tog over next 2 sc) 6 times, sl st to first sc, turn. 48 sts.

Next round: 1 ch (does NOT count as st), (sc2tog over next 2 sc, 1 sc into each of next 6 sc) 6 times, sl st to first sc, turn. 42 sts.

Next round: 1 ch (does NOT count as st), (1 sc into each of next 5 sc, sc2tog over next 2 sc) 6 times, sl st to first sc, turn. 36 sts.

Next round: 1 ch (does NOT count as st), (sc2tog over next 2 sc, 1 sc into each of next 4 sc) 6 times, sl st to first sc, turn. 30 sts.

Next round: 1 ch (does NOT count as st), (1 sc into each of next 3 sc, sc2tog over next 2 sc) 6 times, sl st to first sc, turn. 24 sts.

Next round: 1 ch (does NOT count as st), (sc2tog over next 2 sc, 1 sc into each of next 2 sc) 6 times, sl st to first sc, turn. 18 sts.

Next round: 1 ch (does NOT count as st), (1 sc into next sc, sc2tog over next 2 sc) 6 times, sl st to first sc, turn. 12 sts.

Next round: 1 ch (does NOT count as st), (sc2tog over next 2 sc) 6 times, sl st to first sc, turn. 6 sts.
Work 6 rounds.
Fasten off.

FINISHING

Run a gathering thread around top of last round of Hat, pull up tight and fasten off securely. Fold turn-back to RS around lower edge of Hat.

Booties *(both alike)*

With C2 (2.50 mm) hook, make 24 [27:30:33] ch and join with a sl st to form a ring.

1st round (RS): 1 ch (does NOT count as st), 1 sc into each ch to end, sl st to first sc, turn. 24 [27:30:33] sts.

2nd round: 1 ch (does NOT count as st), 1 sc into each sc to end, sl st to first sc, turn. This round forms sc fabric.

Cont in sc fabric until Bootie measures 2¾ in (7 cm), ending with RS facing for next round.

SHAPE INSTEP

Skip first 9 [10:11:12] sc of next round, join in new ball of yarn to next sc, 1 ch (does NOT count as st), 1 sc into sc where yarn was rejoined, 1 sc into each of next 5 [6:7:8] sc, turn.

Next row: 1 ch (does NOT count as st), 1 sc into each sc to end, turn. 6 [7:8:9] sts.
Rep last row 8 [8:10:10] times more.
Break yarn.

SHAPE FOOT

Return to last complete round worked and cont as follows:

1 ch (does NOT count as st), 1 sc into each of first 9 [10:11:12] sc, 9 [10:11:12] sc evenly up row-end edge of instep, 1 sc into each

of 6 [7:8:9] instep sts, 9 [10:11:12] sc evenly down other row-end edge of instep, 1 sc into each of last 9 [10:11:12] sc, sl st to first sc, turn. 42 [47:52:57] sts.

Work 5 rounds, ending with RS facing for next round.

SHAPE SOLE

Next round: 1 ch (does NOT count as st), *1 sc into each of next 3 [3:4:4] sc, sc2tog over next 2 sc, 1 sc into each of next 11 [13:14:16] sc, sc2tog over next 2 sc, 1 sc into each of next 3 [3:4:4] sc*, (1 sc into next sc) 0 [1:0:1] times, rep from * to * once more, sl st to first sc, turn. 38 [43:48:53] sts. Work 1 round.

Next round: 1 ch (does NOT count as st), *1 sc into each of next 2 [2:3:3] sc, sc2tog over next 2 sc, 1 sc into each of next 11 [13:14:16] sc, sc2tog over next 2 sc, 1 sc into each of next 2 [2:3:3] sc*, (1 sc into next sc) 0 [1:0:1] times, rep from * to * once more, sl st to first sc, turn. 34 [39:44:49] sts.

Next round: 1 ch (does NOT count as st), *1 sc into each of next 1 [1:2:2] sc, sc2tog over next 2 sc, 1 sc into each of next 11 [13:14:16] sc, sc2tog over next 2 sc, 1 sc into each of next 1 [1:2:2] sc*, (1 sc into next sc) 0 [1:0:1] times, rep from * to * once more, sl st to first sc, turn. 30 [35:40:45] sts.

Next round: 1 ch (does NOT count as st), * 1 sc into each of next 0 [0:1:1] sc, sc2tog over next 2 sc, 1 sc into each of next 11 [13:14:16] sc, sc2tog over next 2 sc, 1 sc into each of next 0 [0:1:1] sc*, (1 sc into next sc) 0 [1:0:1] times, rep from * to * once more, sl st to first sc, turn. 26 [31:36:41] sts. Fasten off.

FINISHING

Join sole seam. Fold turn-back to RS around top of Bootie.

Mittens *(both alike)*

With C2 (2.50 mm) hook, make 20 [22:24:26] ch and join with a sl st to form a ring.

1st round (RS): 1 ch (does NOT count as st), 1 sc into each ch to end, sl st to first sc, turn. 20 [22:24:26] sts.

2nd round: 1 ch (does NOT count as st), 1 sc into each sc to end, sl st to first sc, turn. This round forms sc fabric.

Cont in sc fabric until Mitten measures 2½ [2¾:3:3¼] in (6.5 [7:7.5:8] cm).

SHAPE TOP

Next round: 1 ch (does NOT count as st), (sc2tog over next 2 sc, 1 sc into each of next 6 [7:8:9] sc, sc2tog over next 2 sc) twice, sl st to first sc, turn. 16 [18:20:22] sts. Work 1 round.

Next round: 1 ch (does NOT count as st), (sc2tog over next 2 sc, 1 sc into each of next 4 [5:6:7] sc, sc2tog over next 2 sc) twice, sl st to first sc, turn. 12 [14:16:18] sts.

Next round: 1 ch (does NOT count as st), (sc2tog over next 2 sc, 1 sc into each of next 2 [3:4:5] sc, sc2tog over next 2 sc) twice, sl st to first sc, turn. 8 [10:12:14] sts. Fasten off.

FINISHING

Join top seam.

Lacy cardigan

Keep your baby pretty in pink with this soft and fluffy cardigan. The simple lacy stitch, made up of a combination of just doubles and chains, and the minimum of shaping makes it quick and easy to make too. The addition of a classic picot edging completes the look.

MEASUREMENTS

age	0–3	3–6	6–12	12–18	months
chest	16	18	20	22	in
	41	46	51	56	cm
actual chest	19½	21½	23½	25½	in
	50	55	60	65	cm
length	8¼	9¾	11¼	13¼	in
	21	25	30	34	cm
sleeve seam	5	6½	7¾	10½	in
	13	17	20	27	cm

STITCH DIAGRAM

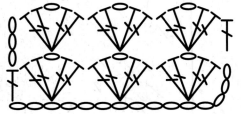

KEY

o	ch
⊤	dc

MATERIALS

• 3 [3:4:4] x 50 g balls of Rowan Kid Classic in Sherbet Dip 850
• Sizes G6 (4.00 mm) and 7 (4.50 mm) crochet hooks
• 5 buttons

ABBREVIATIONS

See page 9.

GAUGE

4 pattern repeats and 7 rows to 4 in (10 cm) measured over pattern using 7 (4.50 mm) hook. Change hook size if necessary to obtain this gauge.

Body

(worked in one piece to armholes)

With 7 (4.50 mm) hook, make 83 [95:99:111] ch loosely.

Foundation row (RS): (2 dc, 1 ch and 2 dc) into 5th ch from hook, *skip 3 ch, (2 dc, 1 ch and 2 dc) into next ch, rep from * to last 2 ch, skip 1 ch, 1 dc into last ch, turn. 102 [117:122:137] sts, 20 [23:24:27] patt reps.

1st row: 3 ch (counts as first dc), skip dc at base of 3 ch and next 2 dc, *(2 dc, 1 ch and 2 dc) into next ch sp**, skip 4 dc, rep from * to end, ending last rep at **, skip 2 dc, 1 dc into top of 3 ch at beg of previous row, turn. This row forms patt.

Work in patt for a further 5 [7:9:11] rows,

ending with WS facing for next row. Body should measure 4 [5:6¼:7½] in (10 [13:16:19] cm).

DIVIDE FOR ARMHOLES

Next row (WS): Patt first 21 [26:26:31] sts ending after "(2 dc, 1 ch and 2 dc) into next ch sp," skip 2 dc, 1 dc into next dc and turn, leaving rem sts unworked.

Work on this set of 22 [27:27:32] sts, 4 [5:5:6] patt reps only for left front.

Work 3 [4:4:5] rows, ending with WS [RS:RS:WS] facing for next row.

SHAPE NECK

1st and 4th sizes only

Next row: Sl st across and into 11th [16th] st,

3 ch (counts as first dc), skip next 2 dc, (2 dc, 1 ch and 2 dc) into next ch sp, patt to end, turn. 12 [17] sts, 2 [3] patt reps.

2nd and 3rd sizes only

Next row: Patt first [11:16] sts ending after "(2 dc, 1 ch and 2 dc) into next ch sp," skip 2 dc, 1 dc into next dc and turn, leaving rem sts unworked. [12:17] sts, [2:3] patt reps.

All sizes

Work 2 [2:3:3] rows.

SHAPE SHOULDER

Fasten off.

SHAPE BACK

Return to last complete row worked, skip next 8 sts, attach yarn to next dc and cont as follows:

Next row: 3 ch (counts as first dc), skip dc at base of 3 ch and next 2 dc, *(2 dc, 1 ch and 2 dc) into next ch sp, skip 4 dc, rep from * 6 [7:8:9] times more, (2 dc, 1 ch and 2 dc) into next ch sp, skip 2 dc, 1 dc into next dc and turn, leaving rem sts unworked.

Work on this set of 42 [47:52:57] sts, 8 [9:10:11] patt reps only for back.

Work 6 [7:8:9] rows.

SHAPE SHOULDER

Fasten off, placing markers either side of center 4 [5:4:5] patt reps to denote back neck.

SHAPE RIGHT FRONT

Return to last complete row worked, skip

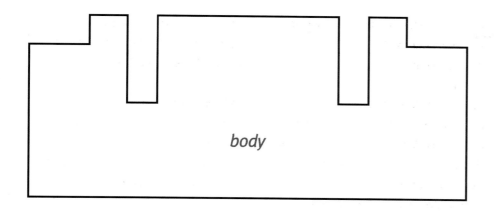

body

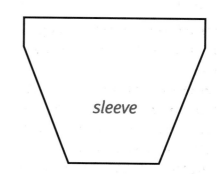

sleeve

next 8 sts, attach yarn to next dc and cont as follows:

Next row: 3 ch (counts as first dc), skip dc at base of 3 ch and next 2 dc, (2 dc, 1 ch and 2 dc) into next ch sp, patt to end, turn. 22 [27:27:32] sts, 4 [5:5:6] patt reps. Complete to match left front, reversing shapings.

Sleeves

With 7 (4.50 mm) hook, make 23 [23:27:27] ch loosely.

Work foundation row as given for Body. 27 [27:32:32] sts, 5 [5:6:6] patt reps.

1st row: 3 ch (counts as first dc), 1 dc into dc at base of 3 ch—1 st increased, skip next 2 dc, *(2 dc, 1 ch and 2 dc) into next ch sp**, skip 4 dc, rep from * to end, ending last rep at **, skip 2 dc, 2 dc into top of 3 ch at beg of previous row—1 st increased, turn.

Working all increases as set by last row, inc 1 st at each end of next 6 [9:7:6] rows, then on foll 0 [0:2:5] alt rows, working inc sts as dcs until there are sufficient to work in patt. 41 [47:52:56] sts.

Work 2 rows.
Fasten off.

Place markers along row-end edges ¾ in (2 cm) down from top of last row to denote top of sleeve seam.

Finishing

Join shoulder seams. Join sleeve seams. Insert sleeves into armholes, matching center of last row of sleeve to shoulder seam and top of sleeve seam to center of sts skipped at underarm.

NECK, FRONT, AND HEM EDGING

With RS facing and using G6 (4.00 mm) hook, rejoin yarn to foundation ch edge directly below left armhole, 1 ch (does NOT count as st), work 1 round of sc evenly around entire hem, front opening and neck edges, working 3 sc into corners, ensuring number of sc worked is divisible by 4 and ending with sl st to first sc, turn.

Mark positions for 5 buttonholes along right front opening edge—first to come 2 in (5 cm) above foundation ch edge, last to

come level with start of neck shaping, and rem 3 buttonholes evenly spaced between.

Next round: 1 ch (does NOT count as st), * 1 sc into each of next 2 sc, 3 ch, sl st to top of sc just worked, 1 sc into each of next 2 sc, rep from * to end, working 3 sc into corner points, making buttonholes to correspond with positions marked by replacing "1 sc into next sc" with "1 ch, skip 1 sc" and ending with sl st to first sc.
Fasten off.

CUFF EDGINGS (BOTH ALIKE)

With RS facing and using G6 (4.00 mm) hook, rejoin yarn to foundation ch edge at base of sleeve seam, 1 ch (does NOT count as st), work 1 round of sc evenly around cuff edge, ensuring number of sc worked is divisible by 4 and ending with sl st to first sc, turn.

Next round: 1 ch (does NOT count as st), * 1 sc into each of next 2 sc, 3 ch, sl st to top of sc just worked, 1 sc into each of next 2 sc, rep from * to end, sl st to first sc.
Fasten off.

Sew on buttons.

Striped hat and scarf

Keep your little one warm on those cold days with this hat and scarf combination. Worked in a soft and fluffy wool yarn, with bright contrasting stripes, it takes almost no time to make! The multicolored tassels add the perfect fun finishing touch.

MEASUREMENTS

age	0–3	3–6	6–12	12–18	months
HAT					
width around head	12¼	13¼	14½	15¾	in
	31	34	37	40	cm
SCARF					
width	4	4¼	4¼	4¾	in
	10	11	11	12	cm
length, excluding tassels	31¼	35½	39¼	43¼	in
	80	90	100	110	cm

STITCH DIAGRAM

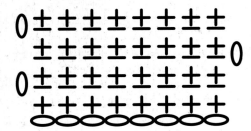

KEY

○ ch
+ sc
± sc worked into front loop only

MATERIALS

• 3 [3:4:4] x 100 g balls Rowan Cocoon in M (Polar 801)
• 1 x 50 g ball of Rowan Pure Wool DK in each of A (Scarlet 041), B (Marine 008) and C (Honey 033)
• Sizes G6 (4.00 mm) and I9 (5.50 mm) crochet hooks

ABBREVIATIONS

See page 9.

GAUGE

14 stitches and 11 rows to 4 in (10 cm) measured over pattern using I9 (5.50 mm) hook and M. Change hook size if necessary to obtain this gauge.

Hat

With I9 (5.50 mm) hook and M, make
44 [48:52:56] ch and join with a sl st to form
a ring.

1st round (RS): 1 ch (does NOT count as st),
1 sc into each ch to end, sl st to first sc, turn.
44 [48:52:56] sts.

Now working into front loops only of sts of
previous rounds, work in patt as follows:

2nd round: 1 ch (does NOT count as st), 1 sc
into each sc to end, sl st to first sc, turn.
This round forms patt.

Work in patt for a further 10 rounds, ending
with RS facing for next round.

4th size only

Next round (RS): 1 ch (does NOT count as st),
(1 sc into each of next 6 sc, sc2tog over next
2 sc, 1 sc into each of next 6 sc) 4 times, sl st
to first sc, turn. 52 sts.

Work 1 round, ending with RS facing for next
round.

3rd and 4th sizes only

Next round (RS): 1 ch (does NOT count as st),
(1 sc into each of next 5 sc, sc2tog over next
2 sc, 1 sc into each of next 6 sc) 4 times, sl st
to first sc, turn. 48 sts.

Work 1 round, ending with RS facing for next
round.

2nd, 3rd and 4th sizes only

Next round (RS): 1 ch (does NOT count as
st), (1 sc into each of next 5 sc, sc2tog over
next 2 sc, 1 sc into each of next 5 sc)
4 times, sl st to first sc, turn. 44 sts.

Work 1 round, ending with RS facing for next
round.

All sizes

Next round (RS): 1 ch (does NOT count as
st), (1 sc into each of next 4 sc, sc2tog over
next 2 sc, 1 sc into each of next 5 sc)
4 times, sl st to first sc, turn. 40 sts.
Work 1 round.

Next round: 1 ch (does NOT count as st),
(1 sc into each of next 4 sc, sc2tog over next
2 sc, 1 sc into each of next 4 sc) 4 times, sl st
to first sc, turn. 36 sts.
Work 1 round.

Next round: 1 ch (does NOT count as st),
(1 sc into each of next 3 sc, sc2tog over next
2 sc, 1 sc into each of next 4 sc) 4 times, sl st
to first sc, turn. 32 sts.
Work 1 round.

Next round: 1 ch (does NOT count as st),
(1 sc into each of next 3 sc, sc2tog over next
2 sc, 1 sc into each of next 3 sc) 4 times, sl st
to first sc, turn. 28 sts.
Work 1 round.

Next round: 1 ch (does NOT count as st),
(1 sc into each of next 2 sc, sc2tog over next
2 sc, 1 sc into each of next 3 sc) 4 times, sl st
to first sc, turn. 24 sts.
Work 1 round.

Next round: 1 ch (does NOT count as st),
(1 sc into each of next 2 sc, sc2tog over next
2 sc, 1 sc into each of next 2 sc) 4 times, sl st
to first sc, turn. 20 sts.
Work 1 round.

Next round: 1 ch (does NOT count as st),
(1 sc into next sc, sc2tog over next 2 sc, 1 sc
into each of next 2 sc) 4 times, sl st to first

sc, turn. 16 sts.
Work 1 round.

Next round: 1 ch (does NOT count as st),
(1 sc into next sc, sc2tog over next 2 sc, 1 sc
into next sc) 4 times, sl st to first sc, turn.
12 sts.
Work 1 round.

Next round: 1 ch (does NOT count as st),
(sc2tog over next 2 sc, 1 sc into next sc)
4 times, sl st to first sc, turn. 8 sts.
Work 1 round.

Next round: 1 ch (does NOT count as st),
(sc2tog over next 2 sc) 4 times, sl st to first
sc, turn. 4 sts.
Work 1 round.
Fasten off.

FINISHING

As patt consists of sc worked into front loops
only of sts of previous rounds, a line is left
around work by the "free" back loops of the
sts. Now work contrast stripes around Hat
by working into these "free" loops. Using A,
B and C at random and placing lines at
random, attach contrast yarn to one "free"
loop. Using G6 (4.00 mm) hook, work a
round of crab st (sc worked from left to right,
instead of right to left) around chosen round
of Hat, ending with sl st to first sc, then
fasten off. Take care not to pull yarn too
tightly as this could distort the work.

Run a gathering thread around top of last
round of Hat, pull up tight and fasten off
securely. Using M, A, B and C together,
make a 4–4½ in (10–12 cm) long tassel and
attach to tip of Hat.

Scarf

With I9 (5.50 mm) hook and M, make
15 [16:17:18] ch.

1st row (RS): 1 sc into 2nd ch from hook, 1 sc
into each ch to end, turn. 14 [15:16:17] sts.
Now working into front loops only of sts of
previous rows, work in patt as follows:

2nd row: 1 ch (does NOT count as st), 1 sc
into each sc to end, turn.
This row forms patt.
Work in patt until Scarf measures
31¼ [35½:39¼:43¼] in (80 [90:100:110] cm),
ending with RS facing for next row.
Fasten off.

FINISHING

As patt consists of sc worked into front loops
only of sts of previous rows, a line is left
across work by the "free" back loops of the
sts. Now work contrast stripes across Scarf
by working into these "free" loops. Using A,
B and C at random and placing lines at
random, attach contrast yarn to one "free"
loop at edge of Scarf. Using G6 (4.00 mm)
hook, work a row of crab st (sc worked from
left to right, instead of right to left) along
chosen row of Scarf, then fasten off. Take
care not to pull yarn too tightly as this could
distort the work.

Run a gathering thread along top of last row
of Scarf, pull up tight and fasten off securely.
Gather foundation ch edge of Scarf in same
way. Using M, A, B, and C together, make
two tassels, each 4–4 ½ in (10–12 cm) long,
and attach to gathered ends of Scarf.

Flared tunic

This cute little flared tunic top is worked in a shaded yarn that creates the subtle stripes as you crochet. It is simple to make and has a useful button opening at the back.

MEASUREMENTS

age	0–3	3–6	6–12	12–18	months
chest	16	18	20	22	in
	41	46	51	56	cm
actual chest	17¼	19½	22	24½	in
	44	50	56	62	cm
length	9¾	11¾	13¾	15¾	in
	25	30	35	40	cm
sleeve seam	5	6¼	7¾	10¼	in
	13	16	20	26	cm

STITCH DIAGRAM

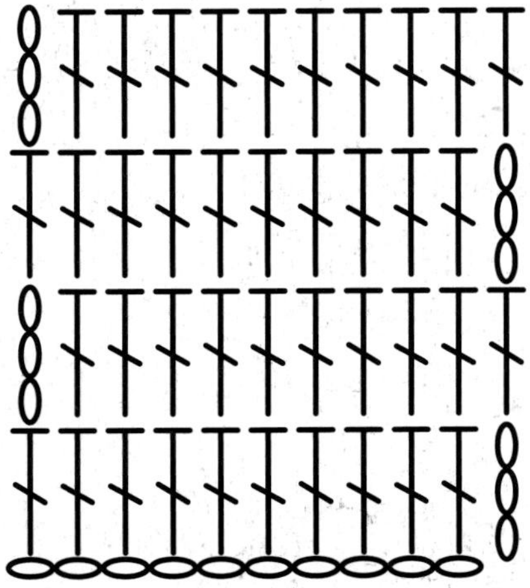

KEY

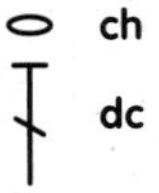

○ ch

† dc

MATERIALS

- 3 [3:4:4] x 50 g balls of Rowan Tapestry in Lakeland 180
- Size E4 (3.50 mm) crochet hook
- 1 button

ABBREVIATIONS

See page 9.

GAUGE

20 stitches and 9½ rows to 4 in (10 cm) measured over double fabric using E4 (3.50 mm) hook.

Change hook size if necessary to obtain this gauge.

Shaping note

Decreases

Work all decreases at beg and ends of rows by working 2 sts together. Work dec at beg of row by working "3 ch (does NOT count as st—remember NOT to work into top of this 3 ch when working next row!), 1 dc into next st—1 st decreased" and work dec at end of row by working "dc2tog over last 2 sts."

To decreases several sts at the end of a row, simply turn before the end of the row, leaving the "decreased" sts unworked. To decrease several sts at the beg of a row, sl st along top of previous row, working a sl st into each "decreased" st and then into what will be first st of next row. Work the "3 ch (counts as first dc)" and complete the row.

Increases

Work all increases at beg and ends of rows by working 2 sts into one st of previous row. Work inc at beg of row by working "3 ch (counts as first dc), 1 dc into st at base of 3 ch—1 st increased" and work inc at end of row by working "2 dc into last st."

Body

(worked in one piece to armholes)
With E4 (3.50 mm) hook, make 106 [126:146:166] ch.
1st row (RS): 1 dc into 4th ch from hook, 1 dc into each ch to end, turn. 104 [124:144:164] sts.
2nd row: 3 ch (counts as first dc), skip dc at base of 3 ch, 1 dc into each dc to end,

working last dc into top of 3 ch at beg of previous row, turn.
Last row forms dc fabric.
Work in dc fabric for a further 4 rows, ending with RS facing for next row.
7th row: 3 ch (counts as first dc), skip dc at base of 3 ch, 1 dc into each of next 1 [4:7:10] dc, dc2tog over next 2 dc, (1 dc into each of next 12 [14:16:18] dc, dc2tog over next 2 dc) 7 times, 1 dc into each of last 2 [5:8:11] sts, turn. 96 [116:136:156] sts.
Work 3 rows.
11th row: 3 ch (counts as first dc), skip dc at base of 3 ch, 1 dc into each of next 4 [7:10:6] dc, dc2tog over next 2 dc, (1 dc into each of next 10 [12:14:18] dc, dc2tog over next 2 dc) 7 times, 1 dc into each of last 5 [8:11:7] sts, turn. 88 [108:128:148] sts.

2nd, 3rd and 4th sizes only

Work 3 rows.
15th row: 3 ch (counts as first dc), skip dc at base of 3 ch, 1 dc into each of next [3:6:9] dc, dc2tog over next 2 dc, (1 dc into each of next [12:14:16] dc, dc2tog over next 2 dc) 7 times, 1 dc into each of last [4:7:10] sts, turn. [100:120:140] sts.

3rd and 4th sizes only

Work 3 rows.
19th row: 3 ch (counts as first dc), skip dc at base of 3 ch, 1 dc into each of next [2:5] dc, dc2tog over next 2 dc, (1 dc into each of next [14:16] dc, dc2tog over next 2 dc) 7 times, 1 dc into each of last [3:6] sts, turn. [112:132] sts.

4th size only

Work 3 rows.
23rd row: 3 ch (counts as first dc), skip dc at base of 3 ch, 1 dc into each of next 8 dc, dc2tog over next 2 dc, (1 dc into each of next 14 dc, dc2tog over next 2 dc) 7 times, 1 dc into each of last 9 sts, turn. 124 sts.

All sizes

Cont straight until Body measures 6 [7½:9:10½] in (15 [19:23:27] cm).

DIVIDE FOR ARMHOLES

Next row: Patt 19 [22:25:28] sts and turn, leaving rem sts unworked.
Work on this set of 19 [22:25:28] sts only for first back.
Dec 1 st at armhole edge of next 3 [4:5:6] rows. 16 [18:20:22]. Work 4 rows.

SHAPE BACK NECK

Dec 10 [11:12:13] sts at back opening edge of next row. 6 [7:8:9] sts.
Dec 1 st at back neck edge of next row. 5 [6:7:8] sts.

SHAPE SHOULDER

Fasten off.

SHAPE FRONT

Return to last complete row worked, skip next 6 sts, attach yarn to next st and cont as follows:
Next row: Patt 38 [44:50:56] sts and turn, leaving rem sts unworked.
Work on this set of 38 [44:50:56] sts only for front.

Dec 1 st at each end of next 3 [4:5:6] rows.
32 [36:40:44] sts.
Work 1 [1:0:0] row.

SHAPE FRONT NECK

Next row: Patt 9 [10:12:13] sts and turn.
Work on this set of 9 [10:12:13] sts only for
first side of neck.
Dec 1 st at neck edge of next 4 [4:5:5]
rows. 5 [6:7:8] sts.

SHAPE SHOULDER

Fasten off.

SHAPE SECOND SIDE OF NECK

Return to last complete row worked before
shaping front neck, skip next 14 [16:16:18]
sts, attach yarn to next dc and cont as
follows:
Next row: Patt to end, turn. 9 [10:12:13] sts.
Complete to match first side of neck,
reversing shapings.

SHAPE SECOND BACK

Return to last complete row worked before
dividing for armholes, skip next 6 sts,
attach yarn to next dc and cont as follows:
Next row: Patt to end, turn. 19 [22:25:28] sts.
Complete to match first back, reversing
shapings.

Sleeves

With E4 (3.50 mm) hook, make 26
[28:30:32] ch.
Work 1st and 2nd rows as given for Body.
24 [26:28:30] sts.

Cont in dc fabric, inc 1 st at each end of
next 5 [4:2:1] rows, then on foll 2 [4:7:7] alt
rows, then on 0 [0:0:2] foll 3rd rows.
38 [42:46:50] sts.
Cont straight until Sleeve measures
5 [6¼:7¼:10¼] in (13 [16:20:26] cm).

SHAPE TOP

Dec 3 sts at each end of next row.
32 [36:40:44] sts.
Dec 1 st at each end of next 6 [7:8:9] rows.
20 [22:24:26] sts.
Fasten off.

Finishing

Join shoulder seams. Join center back
seam, leaving seam open for 2¼ in (6 cm)
at neck edge.

NECK EDGING

With RS facing and using E4 (3.50 mm)
hook, rejoin yarn at right back neck edge
at top of back opening, 1 ch (does NOT
count as st), work 1 round of sc evenly
down right back opening edge, up left
back opening edge, then around entire
neck edge, ending with sl st to first sc, turn.
Next round: 1 ch (does NOT count as st),
1 sc into each sc to top of left side of back
opening, 4 ch (to make a button loop), 1 sc
into each sc, sl st to 1st sc.
Fasten off.

Join sleeve seams. Insert sleeves into
armholes, matching center of last row to
shoulder seam and top of sleeve seam to
center of sts skipped at underarm. Sew on
button.

Furry hat, boots, and mittens

A classic but simple fur, or loop, stitch pattern has been used to create this fun set. Worked in a pure wool yarn, the hat has earflaps to keep out chilly winds and the little pull-on boots and mittens will keep little toes and hands warm too.

MEASUREMENTS

age	0–3	3–6	6–12	12–18	months
HAT					
width around head	13	14	15¼	16½	in
	33	36	39	42	cm
BOOTS					
length of foot	3	3½	4	4¼	in
	8	9	10	11	cm
MITTENS					
width around hand	4	4¼	4¾	5	in
	10	11	12	13	cm

STITCH DIAGRAM

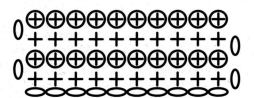

KEY

○ ch
+ sc
⊕ loop 1

MATERIALS

• 2 [2:3:3] x 50 g balls of Rowan Pure Wool DK in Enamel 013
• Size E4 (3.50 mm) crochet hook

ABBREVIATIONS

• **loop 1**—insert hook into next st, form loop of yarn around first finger of left hand and draw both strands of this looped yarn through st, yarn over hook and draw through all 3 loops on hook.
See also page 9.

GAUGE

20 stitches and 24 rows to 4 in (10 cm) measured over pattern using E4 (3.50 mm) hook. Change hook size if necessary to obtain this gauge.

Hat

With E4 (3.50 mm) hook, make 66 [72:78:84] ch and join with a sl st to form a ring.

1st round (RS): 1 ch (does NOT count as st), 1 sc into each ch to end, sl st to first sc, turn. 66 [72:78:84] sts.

2nd round: 1 ch (does NOT count as st), loop 1 into each sc to end, sl st to first st, turn.

3rd round: 1 ch (does NOT count as st), 1 sc into each st to end, sl st to first st, turn. 2nd and 3rd rounds form patt.

Cont in patt until Hat measures 3 [3½:3½:4] in (8 [9:9:10] cm), ending with RS facing for next round.

SHAPE TOP

1st round (RS): 1 ch (does NOT count as st), (sc2tog over next 2 sts, 1 sc into each of next 4 sts) 11 [12:13:14] times, sl st to first st, turn. 55 [60:65:70] sts.
Work 3 rounds.

5th round: 1 ch (does NOT count as st), (sc2tog over next 2 sts, 1 sc into each of next 3 sts) 11 [12:13:14] times, sl st to first st, turn. 44 [48:52:56] sts.
Work 3 rounds.

9th round: 1 ch (does NOT count as st), (sc2tog over next 2 sts, 1 sc into each of next 2 sts) 11 [12:13:14] times, sl st to first st, turn. 33 [36:39:42] sts.
Work 3 rounds.

13th round: 1 ch (does NOT count as st), (sc2tog over next 2 sts, 1 sc into next st) 11 [12:13:14] times, sl st to first st, turn. 22 [24:26:28] sts.

Work 1 round.

15th round: 1 ch (does NOT count as st), (sc2tog over next 2 sts) 11 [12:13:14] times, sl st to first st, turn. 11 [12:13:14] sts.
Work 1 round.

17th round: 1 ch (does NOT count as st), (sc2tog over next 2 sts) 5 [6:6:7] times, (1 sc into last st) 1 [0:1:0] times, sl st to first st, do NOT turn. 6 [6:7:7] sts.

18th round: 1 ch (does NOT count as st), 1 sc into each of next 6 [6:7:7] sc, do NOT turn and do NOT close round with a sl st.
Rep last round 4 times more, ending last round with sl st to next sc.
Fasten off.

FINISHING

Run a gathering thread around top of last round of Hat, pull up tight and fasten off securely.

EARFLAPS (MAKE 2)

With RS facing and E4 (3.50 mm) hook, skip first 8 [9:10:11] sts of foundation ch, attach yarn to next st of foundation ch and cont as follows:

1st row (RS): 1 ch (does NOT count as st), 1 sc into st where yarn was attached, 1 sc into each of next 11 sts of foundation ch, turn. 12 sts.

2nd row: 1 ch (does NOT count as st), 1 sc into each sc to end, turn.

3rd and 4th rows: As 2nd row.

5th row: 1 ch (does NOT count as st), sc2tog over first 2 sc, 1 sc into each sc to last 2 sc, sc2tog over last 2 sc, turn. 10 sts.

6th to 8th rows: As 2nd row.

9th row: As 5th row. 8 sts.

10th row: As 2nd row.

11th to 13th rows: As 5th row. 2 sts.
Fasten off.

Return to foundation ch edge of Hat, skip center front 26 [30:34:38] sts, attach yarn to next st of foundation ch edge and complete second Earflap to match first by working 1st to 13th rows.

LOWER EDGING AND TIES

With RS facing and E4 (3.50 mm) hook,

attach yarn to center back point of foundation ch edge of Hat, 1 ch (does NOT count as st), work evenly in sc along foundation ch edge to first Earflap, then down first side of Earflap to fasten-off point, make 40 ch, 1 sc into 2nd ch from hook, 1 sc into each ch back to fasten-off point of Earflap (to make first Tie), cont in sc around rest of lower edge of Hat and other Earflap, making a second Tie in same way at point of other Earflap, and ending with sl st to first sc. Fasten off. Snip each loop of patt to create fur-like effect.

Boots *(both alike)*

With E4 (3.50 mm) hook, make 9 [10:11:12] ch.

1st round (RS): 2 sc into 2nd ch from hook, 1 sc into each of next 6 [7:8:9] ch, 4 sc into last ch, working back along other side of foundation ch: 1 sc into each of next 6 [7:8:9] ch, 2 sc into last ch (this is same ch as used for first 2 sc), sl st to first sc, turn. 20 [22:24:26] sts.

2nd round: 1 ch (does NOT count as st), 2 sc into each of first 2 sc, 1 sc into each of next 6 [7:8:9] sc, 2 sc into each of next 4 sc, 1 sc into each of next 6 [7:8:9] sc, 2 sc into each of last 2 sc, sl st to first sc, turn. 28 [30:32:34] sts.

3rd round: 1 ch (does NOT count as st), *(1 sc into next sc, 2 sc into next sc) twice, 1 sc into each of next 6 [7:8:9] sc, (2 sc into next sc, 1 sc into next sc) twice, rep from * once more, sl st to first sc, turn. 36 [38:40:42] sts.

4th round: 1 ch (does NOT count as st), *(1 sc into each of next 2 sc, 2 sc into next sc) twice, 1 sc into each of next

6 [7:8:9] sc, (2 sc into next sc, 1 sc into each of next 2 sc) twice, rep from * once more, sl st to first sc, turn. 44 [46:48:50] sts.

These 4 rounds complete base of Boot.

5th round: 1 ch (does NOT count as st), 1 sc into back loop only of each sc to end, sl st to first sc, turn.

6th round: 1 ch (does NOT count as st), loop 1 into each sc to end, sl st to first sc, turn.

7th round: 1 ch (does NOT count as st), 1 sc into each st to end, sl st to first sc, turn.

8th round: As 6th round.

9th round: 1 ch (does NOT count as st), sc2tog over first 2 sts, 1 sc into each st to last 2 sts, sc2tog over last 2 sts, sl st to first st, turn. 42 [44:46:48] sts.

Rep last 2 rounds twice more. 38 [40:42:44] sts.

14th round: As 6th round.

15th round: Fold Boot flat so that tops of last round meet and RS is inside, 1 ch (does NOT count as st), taking care not to catch loops in sts, work 1 sc into each of first 6 sts enclosing last 6 sts of round in these sts (to join seam on top of foot—12 sts decreased), open out work again and turn RS out, 1 sc into each of next 26 [28:30:32] sts, sl st to top of first of these sc, turn. 26 [28:30:32] sts.

16th round: As 6th round.

17th round: As 9th round. 24 [26:28:30] sts.

Now working in rows, not rounds, cont as follows:

18th row (WS): 1 ch (does NOT count as st), loop 1 into each sc to end, turn.

19th row: 1 ch (does NOT count as st), sc2tog over first 2 sts, 1 sc into each st to last 2 sts, sc2tog over last 2 sts, turn. 22 [24:26:28] sts.

Rep last 2 rows once more. 20 [22:24:26] sts.

22nd row: As 18th row.

23rd row: 1 ch (does NOT count as st), 1 sc into each st to end, turn.

24th row: As 18th row.

Fasten off.

FINISHING

With RS facing and E4 (3.50 mm) hook, attach yarn at base of front split (point where work stops being rounds and starts being rows), 1 ch (does NOT count as st), work evenly in sc around entire upper opening edge of Boot, ending with sl st to first sc.

Fasten off.

If desired, snip each loop of patt to create fur-like effect.

Mittens *(both alike)*

With E4 (3.50 mm) hook, make 16 [18:20:22] ch and join with a sl st to form a ring.

1st round (RS): 1 ch (does NOT count as st), 1 sc into each ch to end, sl st to first sc, turn. 16 [18:20:22] sts.

2nd round: 1 ch (does NOT count as st), 1 sc into each sc to end, sl st to first st, turn.

3rd round: 1 ch (does NOT count as st), 2 sc into first sc, 1 sc into each of next

6 [7:8:9] sc, 2 sc into each of next 2 sc, 1 sc into each of next 6 [7:8:9] sc, 2 sc into last sc, sl st to first st, turn. 20 [22:24:26] sts.

4th round: 1 ch (does NOT count as st), loop 1 into each sc to end, sl st to first st, turn.

5th round: 1 ch (does NOT count as st), 1 sc into each st to end, sl st to first st, turn.

4th and 5th rounds form patt.

Cont in patt for a further 9 [9:11:11] rounds, ending with RS facing for next round.

SHAPE TOP

Next round: 1 ch (does NOT count as st), (sc2tog over next 2 sts, 1 sc into each of next 6 [7:8:9] sts, sc2tog over next 2 sts) twice, sl st to first st, turn. 16 [18:20:22] sts.

Work 1 round.

Next round: 1 ch (does NOT count as st), (sc2tog over next 2 sts, 1 sc into each of next 4 [5:6:7] sts, sc2tog over next 2 sts) twice, sl st to first st, turn. 12 [14:16:18] sts.

Work 1 round.

Next round: 1 ch (does NOT count as st), (sc2tog over next 2 sts, 1 sc into each of next 2 [3:4:5] sts, sc2tog over next 2 sts) twice, sl st to first st, turn. 8 [10:12:14] sts.

Work 1 round.

Fasten off.

FINISHING

Join top seam.

If desired, snip each loop of patt to create fur-like effect.

Envelope neck sweater

Made using doubles and single crochet, this little sweater has a wide envelope neck so it is easy to get on and off even the wriggliest baby! Worked in a hand dyed yarn that is mainly cotton, the clever shaded color effect adds interest without the need for complicated stitches.

MEASUREMENTS

age	0–3	3–6	6–12	12–18	months
chest	16	18	20	22	in
	41	46	51	56	cm
actual chest	17¾	20½	22¾	25	in
	45	52	58	64	cm
length	8¼	9¾	11½	13	in
	21	25	29	33	cm
sleeve seam	5	6¼	7¾	10¼	in
	13	16	20	26	cm

MATERIALS
- 3 [4:4:5] x 50 g hanks of Colinette Banyan in Fire 71
- Sizes D3 (3.00 mm) and E4 (3.50 mm) crochet hooks

ABBREVIATIONS
See page 9.

GAUGE
19 stitches and 9 rows to 4 in (10 cm) measured over double fabric using E4 (3.50 mm) hook.
Change hook size if necessary to obtain this gauge.

STITCH DIAGRAM

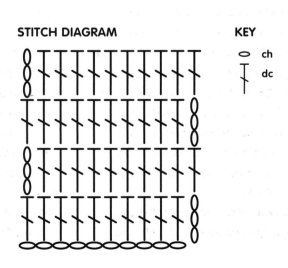

KEY
- ○ ch
- ┬ dc

Shaping note

Decreases

Work all decreases at beg and ends of rows by working 2 sts together. Work dec at beg of row by working "3 ch (does NOT count as st—remember NOT to work into top of this 3 ch when working next row!), 1 dc into next st—1 st decreased" and work dec at end of row by working "dc2tog over last 2 sts."

To decreases several sts at the end of row, simply turn before the end of the row, leaving the "decreased" sts unworked. To decrease several sts at the beg of a row, sl st along top of previous row, working a sl st into each "decreased" st and then into what will be first st of next row. Work the "3 ch (counts as first dc)" and complete the row.

Increases

Work all increases at beg and ends of rows by working 2 sts into one st of previous row. Work inc at beg of row by working "3 ch (counts as first dc), 1 dc into st at base of 3 ch—1 st increased" and work inc at end of row by working "2 dc into last st."

Back

With D3 (3.00 mm) hook, make 44 [50:56:62] ch.

1st row (RS): 1 sc into 2nd ch from hook, 1 sc into each ch to end, turn. 43 [49:55:61] sts.

2nd row: 1 ch (does NOT count as st), 1 sc

into each sc to end, turn.

Rep last row twice more.

Change to E4 (3.50 mm) hook.

5th row: 3 ch (counts as first dc), skip sc at base of 3 ch, 1 dc into each sc to end, turn.

6th row: 3 ch (counts as first dc), skip dc at base of 3 ch, 1 dc into each dc to end, working last dc into top of 3 ch at beg of previous row, turn.

Last row forms dc fabric.

Work in dc fabric until Back measures 4¼ [5½:6½:7¾] in (11 [14:17:20] cm).

SHAPE ARMHOLES

Dec 3 sts at each end of next row.
37 [43:49:55] sts.

Dec 1 st at each end of next 3 [4:5:6] rows.
31 [35:39:43] sts.**

Work 3 rows.

SHAPE BACK NECK

Next row: Patt 7 sts and turn, leaving rem sts unworked.

Work on this set of 7 sts only for first side of neck.

Dec 1 st at neck edge of next 5 rows. 2 sts.
Fasten off.

Place marker along armhole edge 4 rows down from fasten-off point.

SHAPE SECOND SIDE OF NECK

Return to last complete row worked before shaping neck, skip next 17 [21:25:29] sts, attach yarn to next dc and cont as follows:

Next row: Patt to end, turn. 7 sts.

Complete to match first side of neck, reversing shapings.

Front

Work as given for Back to **.

SHAPE FRONT NECK

Next row: Patt 6 sts and turn, leaving rem sts unworked.

Work on this set of 6 sts only for first side of neck.

Dec 1 st at neck edge of next 4 rows.
2 sts.

Fasten off.

back and front

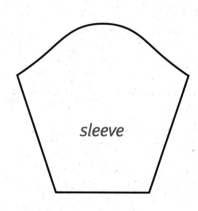

sleeve

Place marker on armhole edge at top of last row.

SHAPE SECOND SIDE OF NECK

Return to last complete row worked before shaping neck, skip next 19 [23:27:31] sts, attach yarn to next dc and cont as follows:

Next row: Patt to end, turn. 6 sts.

Complete to match first side of neck, reversing shapings.

Sleeves

With D3 (3.00 mm) hook, make 24 [26:28:30] ch.

Work 1st to 5th rows as given for Back (remembering to change to E4 (3.50 mm) hook after 4th row). 23 [25:27:29] sts.

Cont in dc fabric, inc 1 st at each end of next 7 [8:9:10] rows. 37 [41:45:49] sts.

Cont straight until Sleeve measures 5 [6¼:7¾:10¼] in (13 [16:20:26] cm).

SHAPE TOP

Dec 3 sts at each end of next row.
31 [35:39:43] sts.
Dec 1 st at each end of next 5 [6:7:8] rows.
21 [23:25:27] sts.
Fasten off.

Finishing

FRONT NECK EDGING

With RS facing and using D3 (3.00 mm) hook, rejoin yarn at top of left front neck, 1 ch (does NOT count as st), work 1 row of sc evenly around entire front neck edge, turn.

Next row: 1 ch (does NOT count as st), 2 sc into first sc, 1 sc into each sc to last sc, 2 sc into last sc.
Fasten off.

BACK NECK EDGING

Work as given for Front Neck Edging.

Lay back neck edge over front so that markers match and sew row-end edges of Back and Back Neck Edging and Front and Front Neck Edging together along armhole edges. Join side seams. Join sleeve seams. Insert sleeves into armholes, matching center of top of last row of sleeves to marked points.

Hat, scarf, and bag

Hot tot! This heirloom set is sure to keep your little one toasty during chilly months ahead. The ruffle effect is stitched up in teams of double crochet to create the highly textured shell-like fringe. The subtle flecks of color in the yarn add visual interest.

MEASUREMENTS

age	0–3	3–6	6–12	12–18	months
HAT					
width around head	13	13¾	15	16	in
	33	35	38	41	cm
SCARF					
width	2¾	2¾	2¾	2¾	in
	7	7	7	7	cm
length (approximate)	27½	31	35	38½	in
	70	79	89	98	cm

STITCH DIAGRAM

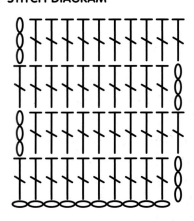

KEY

⬮	ch
⊤	dc

MATERIALS

- 2 [2:3:3] x 110 g hanks of Colinette Jitterbug in Marble 88
- Size C2 (2.50 mm) crochet hook

ABBREVIATIONS

See page 9.

GAUGE

22 stitches and 11 rows to 4 in (10 cm) measured over dc fabric using C2 (2.50 mm) hook.

Change hook size if necessary to obtain this gauge.

Hat

With C2 (2.50 mm) hook, make 4 ch.

1st round (RS): 11 [12:13:14] dc into 4th ch from hook, sl st to top of 3 ch at beg of round, do NOT turn. 12 [13:14:15] sts.

2nd round: 3 ch (counts as first dc), 1 dc into same place as sl st at end of previous round, 2 dc into each dc to end, sl st to top of 3 ch at beg of round, do NOT turn. 24 [26:28:30] sts.

3rd round: 3 ch (counts as first dc), 1 dc into same place as sl st at end of previous round, *1 dc into next dc**, 2 dc into next dc, rep from * to end, ending last rep at **, sl st to top of 3 ch at beg of round, do NOT turn. 36 [39:42:45] sts.

4th round: 3 ch (counts as first dc), 1 dc into same place as sl st at end of previous round, *1 dc into each of next 2 dc**, 2 dc into next dc, rep from * to end, ending last rep at **, sl st to top of 3 ch at beg of round, do NOT turn. 48 [52:56:60] sts.

5th round: 3 ch (counts as first dc), 1 dc into same place as sl st at end of previous round, *1 dc into each of next 3 dc**, 2 dc into next dc, rep from * to end, ending last rep at **, sl st to top of 3 ch at beg of round, do NOT turn. 60 [65:70:75] sts.

6th round: 3 ch (counts as first dc), skip st at base of 3 ch, 1 dc into each of dc to end, sl st to top of 3 ch at beg of round, do NOT turn.

7th round: 3 ch (counts as first dc), 1 dc into same place as sl st at end of previous round, *1 dc into each of next 4 dc**, 2 dc into next dc, rep from * to end, ending last

rep at **, sl st to top of 3 ch at beg of round, do NOT turn. 72 [78:84:90] sts.

Now rep 6th round 7 [7:8:8] times more.

EDGING

1st round: 1 ch (does NOT count as st), 1 sc into each st to end, sl st to first sc.

2nd round: As 1st round.

3rd round: 3 ch (counts as first dc), (2 dc, 1 ch and 3 dc) into same place as sl st at end of previous round, *skip 2 sc**, (3 dc, 1 ch and 3 dc) into next sc, rep from * to end, ending last rep at **, sl st to top of 3 ch at beg of round.

4th round: Sl st across and into first ch sp, 3 ch (counts as first dc), 8 dc into same ch sp, *skip 6 dc**, 9 dc into next ch sp, rep from * to end, ending last rep at **, sl st to top of 3 ch at beg of round.
Fasten off.

Scarf

With C2 (2.50 mm) hook, make 141 [162:183:204] ch.

1st round (RS): 3 dc into 4th ch from hook, 1 dc into each ch to last ch, 8 dc into last ch, now working back along other side of foundation ch: 1 dc into each ch to ch at base of 3 ch at beg of round, 4 dc into same ch as used for 3 dc at beg of round, sl st to top of 3 ch at beg of round, do NOT turn. 288 [330:372:414] sts.

2nd round: 3 ch (counts as first dc), (2 dc, 1 ch and 3 dc) into same place as sl st at end of previous round, *skip 2 dc**, (3 dc, 1 ch and 3 dc) into next dc, rep from * to end,

ending last rep at **, sl st to top of 3 ch at beg of round.

3rd round: Sl st across and into first ch sp, 3 ch (counts as first dc), 8 dc into same ch sp, *skip 6 dc**, 9 dc into next ch sp, rep from * to end, ending last rep at **, sl st to top of 3 ch at beg of round.
Fasten off.

Bag

MAIN SECTION

With C2 (2.50 mm) hook, make 33 ch.

1st round (RS): 1 dc into 4th ch from hook, 1 dc into each of next 28 ch, 4 dc into last ch, now working back along other side of foundation ch: 1 dc into each of next 28 ch, 2 dc into same ch as used for dc at beg of round, sl st to top of 3 ch at beg of round, do NOT turn. 64 sts.

2nd round: 3 ch (counts as first dc), 1 dc into st at base of 3 ch, 1 dc into each of next 30 dc, 2 dc into each of next 2 dc, 1 dc into each of next 30 dc, 2 dc into last dc, sl st to top of 3 ch at beg of round, do NOT turn. 68 sts.

3rd round: 3 ch (counts as first dc), 1 dc into st at base of 3 ch, 1 dc into each of next 32 dc, 2 dc into each of next 2 dc, 1 dc into each of next 32 dc, 2 dc into last dc, sl st to top of 3 ch at beg of round, do NOT turn. 72 sts.

4th round: 3 ch (counts as first dc), 1 dc into st at base of 3 ch, 1 dc into each of next 34 dc, 2 dc into each of next 2 dc, 1 dc into each of next 34 dc, 2 dc into last dc, sl st to top of 3 ch at beg of round, do NOT turn. 76 sts.

5th round: 3 ch (counts as first dc), skip st at base of 3 ch, 1 dc into each dc to end, sl st

to top of 3 ch at beg of round, do NOT turn.

6th to 15th rounds: As 5th round.

16th round: 3 ch (counts as first dc), skip st at base of 3 ch, *(dc2tog over next 2 dc, 1 dc into next dc) 3 times, dc2tog over next 2 dc, 1 dc into each of next 14 dc, dc2tog over next 2 dc, (1 dc into next dc, dc2tog over next 2 dc) 3 times*, 1 dc into each of next 2 dc, rep from * to * once more, 1 dc into last dc, sl st to top of 3 ch at beg of round, turn. 60 sts.

17th round (WS): 1 ch (does NOT count as st), 1 sc into each st to end, sl st to first sc, turn.

18th round: 1 ch (does NOT count as st), working into back loops only of sts of previous round: 1 sc into each sc to end, sl st to first sc, turn.

19th round: 1 ch (does NOT count as st), 1 sc into each st to end, sl st to first sc, do NOT turn.

20th to 31st rounds: As 19th round. Fasten off.

TOP FLOUNCE

With RS facing and with upper opening edge towards you (so that WS of flounce sits against RS of lower section of bag), attach yarn to rem free loop of one sc at side edge of 17th round, 1 ch (does NOT count as st), 1 sc into each sc of 17th round, sl st to first sc, do NOT turn. 60 sts.

2nd round: 3 ch (counts as first dc), (2 dc, 1 ch and 3 dc) into same place as sl st at end of previous round, *skip 2 sc**, (3 dc, 1 ch and 3 dc) into next sc, rep from * to end, ending last rep at **, sl st to top of 3 ch at beg of round.

3rd round: Sl st across and into first ch sp, 3 ch (counts as first dc), 8 dc into same ch sp, *skip 6 dc**, 9 dc into next ch sp, rep from * to end, ending last rep at **, sl st to top of 3 ch at beg of round. Fasten off.

HANDLE

With C2 (2.50 mm) hook, make 9 ch and join with a sl st to form a ring.

1st round (RS): 1 ch (does NOT count as st), 1 sc into each ch to end, do NOT close ring with a sl st and do NOT turn. 9 sts.

2nd round: 1 sc into each sc of previous round.

Rep last round (thereby making a spiralling tube of sc) until Handle measures 10¼ in (26 cm). Fasten off.

Fold last round of Main Section to inside around opening edge, so that top of last round meets top of last dc round. Slip stitch in place. Using photograph as a guide, sew ends of Handle inside upper edge of Bag.

Color block tunic and jacket

Bold blocks of color are combined with a simple textured stitch to create this tunic or jacket! The stitch is really easy to work as it is just a variation of plain single crochet fabric, and the classic cotton yarn means it will be soft and comfortable for baby to wear.

MEASUREMENTS

age	0–3	3–6	6–12	12–18	months
chest	16	18	20	22	in
	41	46	51	56	cm
actual chest	19	20¾	22¾	24¾	in
	48	53	58	63	cm
length	10¼	11¾	13¼	15	in
	26	30	34	38	cm
sleeve seam	5	6¼	7¾	10¼	in
	13	16	20	26	cm

MATERIALS
• Sizes E4 (3.50 mm) and G6 (4.00 mm) crochet hooks

Tunic
• Rowan Handknit Cotton (50 g balls): 1 [2:2:2] balls in A (Rose 332), 1 [2:2:2] balls in B (Delphinium 334), and 1 [2:2:2] balls in C (Antique 333)
• 1 button

Jacket
• Rowan Handknit Cotton (50 g balls): 1 [2:2:2] balls in A (Raffia 330), 1 [2:2:2] balls in B (Slippery 316), and 1 [2:2:2] balls in C (Gooseberry 219)
• Open-ended zipper to fit

ABBREVIATIONS
See page 9.

GAUGE
16 stitches and 16 rows to 4 in (10 cm) measured over pattern using G6 (4.00 mm) hook. Change hook size if necessary to obtain this gauge.

STITCH DIAGRAM

KEY
○ ch
± sc in back loop
∓ sc in front loop

Shaping note

Decreases

Work all decreases at beg and ends of rows by working 2 sts together. Work dec at beg of row by working "1 ch (does NOT count as st), sc2tog over next 2 sts—1 st decreased" and work dec at end of row by working "sc2tog over last 2 sts." As patt consists of sc worked alternately into front and back of sts of previous row, place the sts that make up the "sc2tog" according to the patt.

To decrease several sts at the end of a row, simply turn before the end of the row, leaving the "decreased" sts unworked. To decrease several sts at the beg of a row, sl st along top of previous row, working a sl st into each "decreased" st and then into what will be first st of next row. Work the "1 ch (does NOT count as st) and a sc into st at base of this 1 ch;" then complete the row.

Increases

Work all increases at beg and ends of rows by working 2 sts into one st of previous row. Work inc at beg of row by working "1 ch (does NOT count as st), 2 sc into st at base of 1 ch—1 st increased" and work inc at end of row by working "2 sc into last st."

Tunic back

With E4 (3.50 mm) hook and A, make 39 [43:47:51] ch.
1st row (RS): 1 sc into 2nd ch from hook, 1 sc into each ch to end, turn. 38 [42:46:50] sts.

2nd row: 1 ch (does NOT count as st), 1 sc into each sc to end, turn.
Change to G6 (4.00 mm) hook.
Join in B and now work in patt as follows:
3rd row: Using B, 1 ch (does NOT count as st), 1 sc into back loop only of sc at base of 1 ch, (1 sc into front loop only of next sc, 1 sc into back loop only of next sc) 9 [10:11:12] times, using A, (1 sc into front loop only of next sc, 1 sc into back loop only of next sc) 9 [10:11:12] times, 1 sc into front loop only of last sc, turn.
4th row: Using A, 1 ch (does NOT count as st), 1 sc into back loop only of sc at base of 1 ch, (1 sc into front loop only of next sc, 1 sc into back loop only of next sc) 9 [10:11:12] times, using B, (1 sc into front loop only of next sc, 1 sc into back loop only of next sc) 9 [10:11:12] times, 1 sc into front loop only of last sc, turn.
Last 2 rows form patt and place colors for first section.
Cont as set until Back measures 4 [4¾:5½:6] in (10 [12:14:15] cm), ending with RS facing for next row.
Break off A and join in C.
Using C instead of A, cont straight until Back measures 6¼ [7:7¾:9] in (16 [18:20:23] cm), ending with RS facing for next row.
Break off B and join in A.**
Using A instead of B, cont straight until Back measures 7¾ [9½:11:12½] in (20 [24:28:32] cm), ending with RS facing for next row.

DIVIDE FOR BACK OPENING

Next row: Patt 19 [21:23:25] sts and turn, leaving rem sts unworked.

Work on this set of sts only for first side of neck.
Cont straight until Back measures 10¼ [11¾:13¼:15] in (26 [30:34:38] cm), ending with RS facing for next row.

SHAPE SHOULDER

Fasten off, placing marker 11 [12:13:14] sts in from side seam edge to denote back neck.

Return to last complete row worked before dividing for back opening, attach C to next sc, 1 ch (does NOT count as st), patt to end. 19 [21:23:25] sts.
Complete to match first side.

Tunic front

Work as given for Back to **.
Using A instead of B, cont straight until 8 [8:10:10] rows less have been worked than on Back to fasten-off point, ending with RS facing for next row.

SHAPE FRONT NECK

Next row: Patt 16 [17:19:20] sts and turn, leaving rem sts unworked.
Work on this set of 16 [17:19:20] sts only for first side of neck.
Dec 1 st at neck edge of next 4 rows, then on 1 [1:2:2] foll alt rows. 11 [12:13:14] sts.
Work 1 row, ending with RS facing for next row. Fasten off.

Return to last complete row worked before shaping neck, skip center 6 [8:8:10] sts, attach C to next sc, 1 ch (does NOT count as st), patt to end. 16 [17:19:20] sts.

Complete to match first side, reversing shapings.

Left sleeve

With E4 (3.50 mm) hook and A, make
20 [22:24:26] ch.

Work 1st and 2nd rows as given for Back.
19 [21:23:25] sts.

Change to G6 (4.00 mm) hook.

Break off A and join in C.

Now work in patt as follows:

3rd row: 1 ch (does NOT count as st), 1 sc
into back loop only of sc at base of 1 ch, * 1
sc into front loop only of next sc, 1 sc into
back loop only of next sc, rep from * to
end, turn.

4th row: 1 ch (does NOT count as st), 2 sc
into sc at base of 1 ch—1 st increased, *
1 sc into back loop only of next sc, 1 sc into
front loop only of next sc, rep from * to last
2 sts, 1 sc into back loop only of next sc, 2
sc into last sc—1 st increased, turn.

Last 2 rows form patt and set increases.

Cont in patt, inc 1 st at each end of next
[2nd:2nd:3rd] and 6 [5:3:6] foll alt
[alt:alt:3rd] rows, then on 0 [2:5:3] foll 0
[3rd:3rd:4th] rows, taking inc sts into patt.
35 [39:43:47] sts.

Cont straight until Sleeve measures
5 [6¼:7¾:10¼] in (13 [16:20:26] cm).
Fasten off.

Right sleeve

Work as given for Left Sleeve, but using B in
place of C.

Finishing

Join shoulder seams.

NECK EDGING

With RS facing, using E4 (3.50 mm) hook
and A, attach yarn at top of left back
opening edge, 1 ch (does NOT count as st),
work 1 row of sc evenly around neck edge
to top of right back opening edge, 5 ch (to
make button loop), sl st to last sc.
Fasten off.

Mark points along side seam edges
4¼ [4¾:5:5½] in (11 [12:13:14] cm) either
side of shoulder seams and sew Sleeves to
Back and Front between these points. Join
side and sleeve seams. Sew on button.

Jacket back

Work as given for Back of Tunic to **.
Using A instead of B, cont straight until
Back measures 10¼ [11¾:13¼:15] in
(26 [30:34:38] cm), ending with RS facing for
next row.

Fasten off, placing markers 11 [12:13:14] sts in
from side seam edges to denote back neck.

Left front

With E4 (3.50 mm) hook and A, make
20 [22:24:26] ch.

Work 1st and 2nd rows as given for Back.
19 [21:23:25] sts.

Change to G6 (4.00 mm) hook.

Break off A and join in B.

Now work in patt as follows:

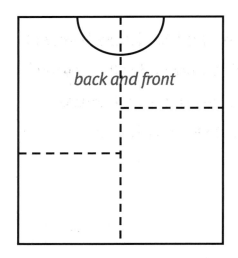

back and front

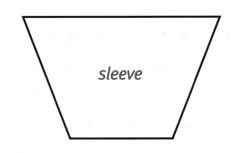

sleeve

3rd row: 1 ch (does NOT count as st), 1 sc into back loop only of sc at base of 1 ch, * 1 sc into front loop only of next sc, 1 sc into back loop only of next sc, rep from * to end, turn.

4th row: 1 ch (does NOT count as st), 1 sc into front loop only of sc at base of 1 ch, * 1 sc into back loop only of next sc, 1 sc into front loop only of next sc, rep from * to end, turn.

Last 2 rows form patt.

Cont as set until Left Front measures 6¼ [7:7¾:9] in (16 [18:20:23] cm), ending with RS facing for next row.

Break off B and join in A.

Cont straight until 8 [8:10:10] rows less have been worked than on Back to fasten-off point, ending with RS facing for next row.

SHAPE NECK

Dec 3 [4:4:5] sts at end of next row. 16 [17:19:20] sts.

Dec 1 st at neck edge of next 4 rows, then on 1 [1:2:2] foll alt rows. 11 [12:13:14] sts.

Work 1 row, ending with RS facing for next row.

Fasten off.

Right front

With E4 (3.50 mm) hook and A, make 20 [22:24:26] ch.

Work 1st and 2nd rows as given for Back. 19 [21:23:25] sts.

Change to G6 (4.00 mm) hook.

Now work in patt as follows:

3rd row: 1 ch (does NOT count as st), 1 sc into front loop only of sc at base of 1 ch, * 1 sc into back loop only of next sc, 1 sc into front loop only of next sc, rep from * to end, turn.

4th row: 1 ch (does NOT count as st), 1 sc into back loop only of sc at base of 1 ch, * 1 sc into front loop only of next sc, 1 sc into back loop only of next sc, rep from * to end, turn.

Last 2 rows form patt.

Cont as set until Right Front measures

4 [4¾:5½:6] in (10 [12:14:15] cm), ending with RS facing for next row.

Break off A and join in C.

Complete to match Left Front, reversing shapings.

Sleeves

Work as given for Sleeves of Tunic.

Finishing

Join shoulder seams.

FRONT AND NECK EDGING

With RS facing, using E4 (3.50 mm) hook and A, attach yarn at base of right front opening edge, 1 ch (does NOT count as st), work 1 row of sc evenly up right front opening edge, around entire neck edge, and down left front opening edge to foundation ch edge, working 3 sc into neck corner points, turn.

Next row: 1 ch (does NOT count as st), 1 sc into each sc to end, working 3 sc into neck corner points and skipping sc as required around neck edge to ensure edging lays flat. Fasten off.

Mark points along side seam edges 4¼ [4¾:5:5½] in (11 [12:13:14] cm) either side of shoulder seams and sew Sleeves to Back and Fronts between these points. Join side and sleeve seams. Insert zipper into front opening.

Blazer

Styled to echo a classic nautical blazer, this little double-breasted jacket is made in a machine-washable wool and cotton mixture yarn. The simple textured stitch combines single and double crochet and the brass buttons complete the stylish look.

MEASUREMENTS

age	0–3	3–6	6–12	12–18	months
chest	16	18	20	22	in
	41	46	51	56	cm
actual chest	18½	21¼	24	26¾	in
	47	54	61	68	cm
length	9	10½	12¼	13¾	in
	23	27	31	35	cm
sleeve seam	4¾	6	7½	9	in
	12	15	19	23	cm

MATERIALS

• 4 [4:5:5] x 50 g balls of Rowan Wool Cotton in French Navy 909
• Size E4 (3.50 mm) crochet hook
• 4 buttons

ABBREVIATIONS

See page 9.

GAUGE

17 stitches and 14 rows to 4 in (10 cm) measured over pattern using E4 (3.50 mm) hook.

Change hook size if necessary to obtain this gauge.

STITCH DIAGRAM

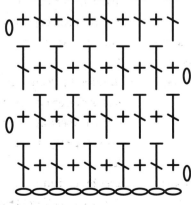

KEY

○ ch
+ sc
T dc

Shaping note

Decreases

To dec 1 st at beg of row, work: 1 sl st into each of first 2 sts, make appropriate turning ch—which may or may not count as st depending on point in patt, if it DOES count as a st, skip st at base of turning ch, but if it DOES NOT count as st, work appropriate st into st at base of turning ch.

To dec 1 st at end of row, simply turn one st before end of row, leaving decreased st unworked.

To work a multiple dec at beg of row, break and fasten off yarn. Skip the appropriate number of sts and rejoin yarn to next st, make appropriate turning ch (depending on point in patt) and complete row. To work a multiple dec at the end of a row, simply turn the required number of sts before the end of the row, leaving the "decreased" sts unworked.

Increases

Work all increases at beg and ends of rows by working 2 sts into one st of previous row. Remember patt alternates between a sc and a dc and work sts accordingly. If first st of new row should be a sc, inc will be "3 ch (counts as dc), 1 sc into st at base of 3 ch." If first st of new row should be a dc, inc will be "1 ch (does NOT count as st, (1 sc and 1 dc) into st at base of 1 ch."

Pattern note

As there are no edgings on this garment, it is important to keep the outer finished edges neat.

Body

(worked in one piece to armholes)
With E4 (3.50 mm) hook, make 93 [107:121:135] ch.
1st row (RS): 1 sc into 2nd ch from hook, * 1 dc into next ch**, 1 sc into next ch, rep from * to end, ending last rep at **, turn. 92 [106:120:134] sts.

Now work in patt as follows:
2nd row: 1 ch (does NOT count as st), 1 sc into dc at base of 1 ch, *1 dc into next sc **, 1 sc into next dc, rep from * to end, ending last rep at **, turn.
This row forms patt.
Work in patt for a further 4 [6:8:10] rows, ending with RS facing for next row.

Girl's version only
Next row (buttonhole row) (RS): Patt 2 sts, 1 ch, skip 1 st (to make first buttonhole of first pair—on next row, work appropriate st into this ch sp), patt 6 [8:10:12] sts, 1 ch, skip 1 st (to make second buttonhole of first pair—on next row, work appropriate st into this ch sp), patt to end, turn.

Boy's version only
Next row (buttonhole row) (RS): Patt to last 10 [12:14:16] sts, 1 ch, skip 1 st (to make first buttonhole of first pair—on next row, work appropriate st into this ch sp), patt 6 [8:10:12] sts, 1 ch, skip 1 st (to make second buttonhole of first pair—on next row,

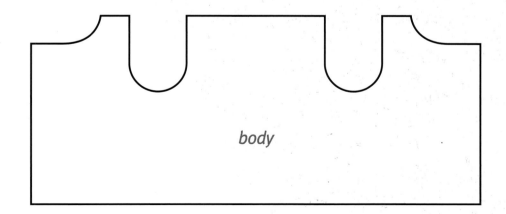

body

sleeve

work appropriate st into this ch sp), patt last 2 sts, turn.

Both versions

Patt a further 7 [9:9:11] rows, ending with RS facing for next row.

Rep the buttonhole row once more.

Cont straight until Body measures 5 [6¼:7½:8½] in (13 [16:19:22] cm), ending with RS facing for next row.

DIVIDE FOR ARMHOLES

Next row (RS): Patt first 24 [28:31:35] sts and turn, leaving rem sts unworked.

Work on this set of 24 [28:31:35] sts only for right front.

Keeping patt correct, dec 1 st at armhole edge of next 4 [5:6:7] rows. 20 [23:25:28] sts.

Cont straight until armhole measures 2¼ [2¾:2¾:3] in (6 [7:7:8] cm), ending with RS facing for next row.

SHAPE NECK

Keeping patt correct, dec 10 [12:13:15] sts at front opening edge of next row. 10 [11:12:13] sts.

Dec 1 st at neck edge of next 4 rows, then on foll 0 [0:1:1] alt row. 6 [7:7:8] sts.

Cont straight until armhole measures 4 [4¼:4¾:5] in (10 [11:12:13] cm), ending with RS facing for next row.

SHAPE SHOULDER

Fasten off.

SHAPE BACK

Return to last complete row worked, skip next 4 [4:6:6] sts, attach yarn to next st, patt 36 [42:46:52] sts and turn, leaving rem sts unworked.

Work on this set of 36 [42:46:52] sts only for back.

Keeping patt correct, dec 1 st at each end of next 4 [5:6:7] rows. 28 [32:34:38] sts.

Cont straight until armhole measures 4 [4¼:4¾:5] in (10 [11:12:13] cm), ending with RS facing for next row.

SHAPE SHOULDER

Fasten off, placing markers either side of center 16 [18:20:22] sts to denote back neck.

SHAPE LEFT FRONT

Return to last complete row worked, skip next 4 [4:6:6] sts, attach yarn to next st, patt to end. 24 [28:31:35] sts.

Complete to match right front, reversing shapings.

Sleeves

With E4 (3.50 mm) hook, make 21 [23:25:27] ch.

Work 1st and 2nd rows as given for Body. 20 [22:24:26] sts.

Cont in patt, shaping sides by inc 1 st at each end of next and foll 5 [4:3:2] alt rows, then on 0 [2:4:6] foll 3rd rows. 32 [36:40:44] sts.

Cont straight until Sleeve measures 4¾ [6:7½:9] in (12 [15:19:23] cm), ending with RS facing for next row.

SHAPE TOP

Keeping patt correct, dec 2 [2:3:3] sts at each end of next row. 28 [32:34:38] sts.

Dec 1 st at each end of next 9 [11:11:13] rows, ending with RS facing for next row. 10 [10:12:12] sts.

Fasten off.

Finishing

Join shoulder seams.

COLLAR

With E4 (3.50 mm) hook, make 39 [43:49:53] ch.

Work 1st and 2nd rows as given for Body. 38 [42:48:52] sts.

Cont in patt for 4 rows, ending with RS facing for next row.

Place markers at both ends of last row.

Dec 5 [6:7:7] sts at end of next 2 rows, then 6 [6:7:8] sts at end of next 2 rows. 16 [18:20:22] sts.

Fasten off.

Mark points along neck shaping 6 [7:8:9] sts in from front opening edges. Matching markers, sew shaped upper edge of Collar to neck edge between these points. Join sleeve seams. Matching top of sleeve seam to center of sts skipped at underarm and center of last row of Sleeve to shoulder seam, sew Sleeves into armholes. Sew on buttons so that front opening edges overlap by 12 [14:16:18] sts.

Striped sweater

Bold stripes of color add the interest to this classic sweater, worked in doubles. The buttoned shoulder opening makes it easy to put on and take off. Choose classic shades of blue as here, or soft and pretty pastels for a little girl.

MEASUREMENTS

age	0–3	3–6	6–12	12–18	months
chest	16	18	20	22	in
	41	46	51	56	cm
actual chest	18	20¾	23¼	25½	in
	46	53	59	65	cm
length	8¼	9¾	11½	13	in
	21	25	29	33	cm
sleeve seam	4¾	6	7½	9	in
	12	15	19	23	cm

MATERIALS

• Rowan RYC Cashsoft DK (50 g balls): 1 [2:2:2] balls in A (Navy 514), 1 [1:2:2] balls in B (Ballad Blue 508), and 1 [1:2:2] balls in C (Cream 500)
• Size E4 (3.50 mm) crochet hook
• 2 buttons

ABBREVIATIONS

See page 9.

GAUGE

19 stitches and 9½ rows to 4 in (10 cm) measured over double fabric using E4 (3.50 mm) hook.
Change hook size if necessary to obtain this gauge.

STITCH DIAGRAM

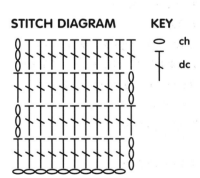

KEY

○ ch

⊤ dc

Shaping note

Decreases

Work all decreases at beg and ends of rows by working 2 sts together. Work dec at beg of row by working "3 ch (does NOT count as st—remember NOT to work into top of this 3 ch when working next row!), 1 dc into next st—1 st decreased" and work dec at end of row by working "dc2tog over last 2 sts."

To decreases several sts at the end of a row, simply turn before the end of the row, leaving the "decreased" sts unworked. To decrease several sts at the beg of a row, sl st along top of previous row, working a sl st into each "decreased" st and then into what will be first st of next row. Work the "3 ch (counts as first dc)" and then complete the row.

Increases

Work all increases at beg and ends of rounds by working 2 sts into one st of previous round. Work inc at beg of round by working "3 ch (counts as first dc), 1 dc into st at base of 3 ch—1 st increased" and work inc at end of round by working "2 dc into last st."

Stripe sequence

After first 3 rounds have been worked, work in stripes as follows:
4 rounds (or rows) using B.
2 rounds (or rows) using C.
4 rounds (or rows) using A.
2 rounds (or rows) using B.
4 rounds (or rows) using C.
2 rounds (or rows) using A.
These 18 rounds (or rows) form stripe sequence and are repeated as required.

Body

(worked in one piece to armholes)

With E4 (3.50 mm) hook and A, make 88 [100:112:124] ch and join with a sl st to form a ring.

1st round (WS): 1 ch (does NOT count as st), 1 sc into each ch to end, sl st to first sc, turn. 88 [100:112:124] sts.

2nd round: 1 ch (does NOT count as st), 1 sc into each sc to end, sl st to first sc, turn. Now work in dc fabric as follows:

3rd round (WS): 3 ch (counts as first dc), skip st at base of 3 ch, 1 dc into each st to end, sl st to top of 3 ch at beg of round, turn. This round forms dc fabric.

Joining in colors as required, now work in dc fabric in stripe sequence (see above and starting with 4 rounds using B) for a further 8 [11:14:17] rounds, ending after 2 [1:2:1] rounds using A [B:C:A]. (A total of 11 [14:17:20] rounds completed from foundation ch edge.)

SHAPE BACK

Next row: Sl st across first 3 sts of next "round" and into 4th st, 3 ch (counts as first dc), skip st at base of 3 ch, 1 dc into each of next 37 [43:49:55] dc and turn, leaving rem sts unworked.

Now working backwards and forwards in rows, not rounds, but keeping stripes correct, work on this set of 38 [44:50:56] sts only for back as follows:

Dec 1 st at each end of next 4 [5:6:7] rows. 30 [34:38:42] sts.

Work a further 5 rows, ending after 2 [4:2:2] rows using A [B:A:B] and with RS facing for next row. Armhole should measure approx 4 [4¼:4¾:5] in (10 [11:12:13] cm).

SHAPE SHOULDERS

Fasten off, placing markers either side of center 20 [22:24:26] sts to denote back neck, and at ends of last row to denote shoulder points.

LEFT BACK SHOULDER BUTTON BAND

With RS facing, skip first 25 [28:31:34] sts of next row, keeping stripe sequence correct attach appropriate yarn to next st, 1 ch (does NOT count as st), 1 sc into st at base of 1 ch, 1 sc into each of last 4 [5:6:7] sts, turn. 5 [6:7:8] sts.

Next row: 1 ch (does NOT count as st), 1 sc into each st to end.
Fasten off.

SHAPE FRONT

Return to last complete round worked, skip next 6 sts, attach appropriate yarn to next st, 3 ch (counts as first dc), skip st at base of 3 ch, 1 dc into each of next 37 [43:49:55] dc and turn, leaving rem sts unworked.

Dec 1 st at each end of next 4 [5:6:7] rows. 30 [34:38:42] sts.

SHAPE FRONT NECK

Next row (WS): 3 ch (counts as first dc), skip

dc at base of 3 ch, 1 dc into each of next 7 [8:9:10] dc and turn, leaving rem sts unworked. 8 [9:10:11] sts.
Dec 1 st at neck edge of next 3 rows. 5 [6:7:8] sts.
Work 1 row, ending after 2 [4:2:2] rows using A [B:A:B] and with RS facing for next row.

SHAPE SHOULDER

Fasten off.

SHAPE SECOND SIDE OF NECK

Return to last complete row worked, skip next 14 [16:18:20] sts, attach appropriate yarn to next st, 3 ch (counts as first dc), skip dc at base of 3 ch, 1 dc into each of last 7 [8:9:10] dc, turn. 8 [9:10:11] sts.
Dec 1 st at neck edge of next 3 rows. 5 [6:7:8] sts.

LEFT FRONT SHOULDER BUTTONHOLE BAND

Using A [B:A:B] only, complete this side of neck as follows:
Next row (WS): 1 ch (does NOT count as st), 1 sc into each of first 2 [2:3:3] sts, 1 ch, skip 1 st (to make a buttonhole), 1 sc into each of last 2 [3:3:4] sts, turn.
Next row: 1 ch (does NOT count as st), 1 sc into each sc and ch sp to end.
Fasten off.

Sleeves

With E4 (3.50 mm) hook and C, make 22 [24:26:28] ch and join with a sl st to form a ring.

Work 1st and 2nd rounds as given for Body. 22 [24:26:28] sts.
Starting with 1 [0:1:2] further rounds using C and then 2 rounds using A, cont in dc fabric in stripe sequence as given for Body as follows:
Inc 1 st at each end of next 7 [7:5:3] rounds, then on foll 1 [2:5:8] alt rounds. 38 [42:46:50] sts.
Work a further 2 rounds, ending after 2 [1:2:1] rounds using A [B:C:A].
Sleeve should measure 4¾ [6:7½:9] in (12 [15:19:23] cm).

SHAPE TOP

Keeping stripes correct but now working backwards and forwards in rows, not rounds, dec 3 sts at each end of next row. 32 [36:40:44] sts.
Dec 1 st at each end of next 5 rows. 22 [26:30:34] sts.
Fasten off.

Finishing

Join right shoulder seam. Lay left front shoulder buttonhole band over left back shoulder button band so that top of buttonhole band matches top of last dc row of Back and sew together at armhole edge.

NECKBAND

With RS facing, E4 (3.50 mm) hook and C [A:B:A], attach yarn at top of neck edge of left front shoulder buttonhole border, 1 ch (does NOT count as st), work 1 row of sc evenly around entire neck edge, ending at top of last row of back neck shoulder button band, turn.
Skipping sc as required to ensure Neckband lays flat, cont as follows:
Next row: 1 ch (does NOT count as st), 1 sc into each sc to last 3 sc, 1 ch, skip 1 sc (to make 2nd buttonhole), 1 sc into each of last 2 sc, turn.
Next row: 1 ch (does NOT count as st), 1 sc into each sc or ch sp to end.
Fasten off.

Matching skipped sts at underarm and center of last row of Sleeve to shoulder seam, sew Sleeves into armholes. Sew on buttons to correspond with buttonholes.

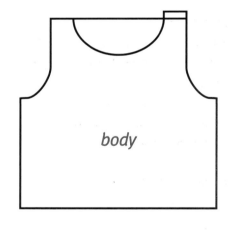

body

sleeve

Rabbit

This cute little rabbit is sure to charm any tiny tot. Simply made in single crochet, using a pure wool yarn, his arms and legs are just the right size for baby's tiny hands to hold!

MEASUREMENT
Complete Rabbit measures approx 14 in (36 cm) from tips of ears to base of feet

MATERIALS
• Rowan Pure Wool DK (50 g balls): 2 balls in A (Enamel 013) and 1 ball in B (Sugar Pink 038)
• E4 (3.50 mm) crochet hook
• Oddment of blue yarn for eyes
• Washable toy filling

ABBREVIATIONS
See page 9.

GAUGE
19 stitches and 20 rows to 4 in (10 cm) measured over single crochet fabric using E4 (3.50 mm) hook.
Change hook size if necessary to obtain this gauge.

STITCH DIAGRAM

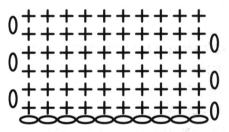

KEY
⊙ ch
+ sc

Feet *(make two)*

With E4 (3.50 mm) hook and A, make 6 ch and fasten off (6 "V" shapes visible along length).

Attach A to 4th st from beginning of ch and cont as follows:

1st round (RS): 1 ch (does NOT count as st), 1 sc into ch at base of 1 ch, 1 sc into next ch, 2 sc into end ch, working back along other side of ch: 1 sc into each of next 4 ch, 2 sc into last ch, working back along rem section of first side of ch: 1 sc into each of next 2 ch, sl st to first sc, turn. 12 sts.

2nd round: Using A 1 ch (does NOT count as st), 2 sc into first sc, 1 sc into next sc, 2 sc into each of next 2 sc, using B 1 sc into each of next 4 sc, using A 2 sc into each of next 2 sc, 1 sc into next sc, 2 sc into last sc, sl st to first sc, turn. 18 sts.

3rd round: Using A 1 ch (does NOT count as st), 1 sc into each of first 4 sc, 2 sc into each of next 2 sc, using B 1 sc into each of next 6 sc, using A 2 sc into each of next 2 sc, 1 sc into each of last 4 sc, sl st to first sc, turn. 22 sts.

4th round: Using A 1 ch (does NOT count as st), 1 sc into each of first 7 sc, using B 1 sc into each of next 8 sc, using A 1 sc into each of last 7 sc, sl st to first sc, turn.

5th to 7th rounds: As 4th round.

8th round: Using A 1 ch (does NOT count as st), 1 sc into each of first 8 sc, using B 1 sc into each of next 6 sc, using A 1 sc into each of last 8 sc, sl st to first sc, turn.

Now working in rows, not rounds, cont as follows:

9th row: Using A 1 ch (does NOT count as st), sc2tog over first 2 sc, 1 sc into each of next 2 sc, (sc2tog over next 2 sc) twice, using B 1 sc into each of next 6 sc, using A (sc2tog over next 2 sc) twice, 1 sc into each of next 2 sc, sc2tog over last 2 sc, turn. 16 sts.

10th row: Using A 1 ch (does NOT count as st), sc2tog over first 2 sc, 1 sc into each of next 4 sc, using B 1 sc into each of next 4 sc, using A 1 sc into each of next 4 sc, sc2tog over last 2 sc, turn. 14 sts.

11th row: Using A 1 ch (does NOT count as st), 1 sc into first sc, (sc2tog over next 2 sc) twice, 1 sc into next sc, using B 1 sc into each of next 2 sc, using A 1 sc into next sc, (sc2tog over next 2 sc) twice, 1 sc into last sc, turn. 10 sts.

Break off B and cont using A only.

Now working in rounds, not rows, cont as follows:

12th round: 1 ch (does NOT count as st), 1 sc into first sc, sc2tog over same st as already worked into and next sc, sc2tog over next 2 sc, 1 sc into each of next 2 sc, (sc2tog over next 2 sc) twice, 1 sc into same place as used for last "leg" of last sc2tog—this is last st of round, sl st to first sc.

Fasten off.

Fold Foot flat with "hole" for Leg at center and join seam across back of Foot.

Legs *(make two)*

With E4 (3.50 mm) hook and A, attach yarn to back of "hole" left in Foot for Leg and cont as follows:

1st round (RS): 1 ch (does NOT count as st), work 9 sc evenly around "hole," sl st to first sc, turn. 9 sts.

2nd round: 1 ch (does NOT count as st), 1 sc into each sc to end, sl st to first sc, turn. Insert toy filling into Foot so Foot is quite firmly filled.

3rd to 20th rounds: As 2nd round.

Fasten off.

Insert toy filling into Leg so Leg is quite softly filled. Fold top of Leg flat so that Foot section extends forwards from fold.

Body

BASE

With E4 (3.50 mm) hook and A, make 10 ch.

1st row: 1 sc into 2nd ch from hook, 1 sc into each ch to end, turn. 9 sts.

2nd row: 1 ch (does NOT count as st), 2 sc into first sc, 1 sc into each of next 7 sc, 2 sc into last sc, turn. 11 sts.

3rd row: 1 ch (does NOT count as st), 1 sc into each sc to end, turn.

4th row: As 3rd row.

5th row: 1 ch (does NOT count as st), sc2tog over first 2 sc, 1 sc into each sc to last 2 sc, sc2tog over last 2 sc, turn. 9 sts.

6th to 8th rows: As 5th row. 3 sts.

Fasten off.

Base is a triangular shape—foundation ch edge is front edge and last row is center back edge.

BODY

With RS facing, E4 (3.50 mm) hook and A, attach yarn at center of last row, 1 ch (does

NOT count as st), work 9 sc evenly along one shaped edge to foundation ch edge, holding Legs against RS of Base, work 1 sc into each of first 4 foundation ch enclosing top folded edge of Leg in sts (make sure Foot points forwards!), 1 sc into next foundation ch, now work 1 sc into each of last 4 foundation ch enclosing top folded edge of other Leg in sts, now work 9 sc evenly up other shaped edge of Base to point where yarn was rejoined, sl st to first sc, turn. 27 sts.

1st round (WS): 1 ch (does NOT count as st), 2 sc into first sc, (1 sc into each of next 7 sc, 2 sc into each of next 2 sc) twice, 1 sc into each of next 7 sc, 2 sc into last sc, sl st to first sc, turn. 33 sts.

2nd round: Using A 1 ch (does NOT count as st), 2 sc into first sc, 1 sc into each of next 9 sc, 2 sc into each of next 2 sc, 1 sc into next sc, using B 1 sc into each of next 7 sc, using A 1 sc into next sc, 2 sc into each of next 2 sc, 1 sc into each of next 9 sc, 2 sc into last sc, sl st to first sc, turn. 39 sts.

3rd round: Using A 1 ch (does NOT count as st), 1 sc into each of first 15 sc, using B 1 sc into each of next 9 sc, using A 1 sc into each of last 15 sc, sl st to first sc, turn.

4th to 6th rounds: As 3rd round.

7th round: Using A 1 ch (does NOT count as st), 1 sc into each of first 16 sc, using B 1 sc into each of next 7 sc, using A 1 sc into each of last 16 sc, sl st to first sc, turn.

8th round: Using A 1 ch (does NOT count as st), sc2tog over first 2 sc, 1 sc into each of next 9 sc, (sc2tog over next 2 sc) twice, 1 sc into next sc, using B 1 sc into each of next 7 sc, using A 1 sc into next sc, (sc2tog over next 2 sc) twice, 1 sc into each of next 9 sc, sc2tog over last 2 sc, sl st to first sc, turn. 33 sts.

9th round: Using A 1 ch (does NOT count as st), 1 sc into each of first 14 sc, using B 1 sc into each of next 5 sc, using A 1 sc into each of last 14 sc, sl st to first sc, turn.

10th round: Using A 1 ch (does NOT count as st), sc2tog over first 2 sc, 1 sc into each of next 7 sc, (sc2tog over next 2 sc) twice, 1 sc into next sc, using B 1 sc into each of next 5 sc, using A 1 sc into next sc, (sc2tog over next 2 sc) twice, 1 sc into each of next 7 sc, sc2tog over last 2 sc, sl st to first sc, turn. 27 sts.

11th round: Using A 1 ch (does NOT count as st), 1 sc into each of first 12 sc, using B 1 sc into each of next 3 sc, using A 1 sc into each of last 12 sc, sl st to first sc, turn.

12th round: Using A 1 ch (does NOT count as st), sc2tog over first 2 sc, 1 sc into each of next 5 sc, (sc2tog over next 2 sc) twice, 1 sc into next sc, using B 1 sc into each of next 3 sc, using A 1 sc into next sc, (sc2tog over next 2 sc) twice, 1 sc into each of next 5 sc, sc2tog over last 2 sc, sl st to first sc, turn. 21 sts.

Break off B and cont using A only.

13th round: 1 ch (does NOT count as st), 1 sc into each sc to end, sl st to first sc, turn.

14th round: 1 ch (does NOT count as st), sc2tog over first 2 sc, 1 sc into each of next 3 sc, (sc2tog over next 2 sc) twice, 1 sc into each of next 3 sc, (sc2tog over next 2 sc) twice, 1 sc into each of next 3 sc, sc2tog over last 2 sc, sl st to first sc, turn. 15 sts.

15th round: As 13th round.

Fasten off.

Insert toy filling so that Body is firmly filled.

Head

With E4 (3.50 mm) hook and A, make 12 ch and join with a sl st to form a ring.

1st round (RS): 1 ch (does NOT count as st), 1 sc into each ch to end, sl st to first sc, turn. 12 sts.

2nd round: 1 ch (does NOT count as st), 1 sc into each of first 2 sc, 2 sc into each of next 2 sc, 1 sc into each of next 4 sc, 2 sc into each of next 2 sc, 1 sc into each of last 2 sc, sl st to first sc, turn. 16 sts.

3rd round: 1 ch (does NOT count as st), 1 sc into each of first 3 sc, 2 sc into each of next 2 sc, 1 sc into each of next 6 sc, 2 sc into each of next 2 sc, 1 sc into each of last 3 sc, sl st to first sc, turn. 20 sts.

4th round: 1 ch (does NOT count as st), 2 sc into first sc, 1 sc into each of next 3 sc, 2 sc into each of next 2 sc, 1 sc into each of next 8 sc, 2 sc into each of next 2 sc, 1 sc into each of next 3 sc, 2 sc into last sc, sl st to first sc, turn. 26 sts.

5th round: 1 ch (does NOT count as st), 1 sc into each sc to end, sl st to first sc, turn.

6th to 8th rounds: As 5th round.

9th round: 1 ch (does NOT count as st), 1 sc into each of first 5 sc, (sc2tog over next 2 sc) twice, 1 sc into each of next 8 sc, (sc2tog over next 2 sc) twice, 1 sc into each of last 5 sc, sl st to first sc, turn. 22 sts.

10th round: As 5th round.

11th round: 1 ch (does NOT count as st), sc2tog over first 2 sc, 1 sc into each of next 2 sc, (sc2tog over next 2 sc) twice, 1 sc into each of next 6 sc, (sc2tog over next 2 sc) twice, 1 sc into each of next 2 sc, sc2tog over last 2 sc, sl st to first sc, turn. 16 sts.

12th round: 1 ch (does NOT count as st), 1 sc into each of first 2 sc, (sc2tog over next 2 sc) twice, 1 sc into each of next 4 sc, (sc2tog over next 2 sc) twice, 1 sc into each of last 2 sc, sl st to first sc, turn. 12 sts.

Fasten off.

Fold Head flat with beg and end of rounds running up center back and close top edge. Insert toy filling so Head is firmly filled, then sew foundation ch edge to top of Body, inserting a little more toy filling into neck section.

Arms (make two)

With E4 (3.50 mm) hook and A, make 2 ch.

1st round (RS): 6 sc into 2nd ch from hook, sl st to first sc, turn. 6 sts.

2nd round: 1 ch (does NOT count as st), 2 sc into each of first 2 sc, 1 sc into next sc, 2 sc into each of next 2 sc, 1 sc into last sc, sl st to first sc, turn. 10 sts.

3rd round: 1 ch (does NOT count as st), 1 sc into first sc, 2 sc into each of next 2 sc, 1 sc into each of next 3 sc, 2 sc into each of next 2 sc, 1 sc into each of last 2 sc, sl st to first sc, turn. 14 sts.

4th round: 1 ch (does NOT count as st), 1 sc into each sc to end, sl st to first sc, turn.

5th to 10th rounds: As 4th round.

11th round: 1 ch (does NOT count as st), 1 sc into first sc, (sc2tog over next 2 sc) twice, 1 sc into each of next 3 sc, (sc2tog over next 2 sc) twice, 1 sc into each of last 2 sc, sl st to first sc, turn. 10 sts.

12th to 16th rounds: As 4th round.

Now working in rows, not rounds, cont as follows:

17th row: 1 ch (does NOT count as st), sc2tog over first 2 sc, 1 sc into each sc to last 2 sc, sc2tog over last 2 sc, turn. 8 sts.

18th and 19th rows: As 17th row. 4 sts.

20th row: 1 ch (does NOT count as st), (sc2tog over next 2 sc) twice. 2 sts.

Fasten off.

Insert toy filling into Arm so Arm is quite softly filled. Fold top of Arm flat so that shaped edges form a diagonal line. Using photograph as a guide, sew Arms to Body just back from chest patch.

Ears (make two)

With E4 (3.50 mm) hook and A, make 2 ch.

1st round (RS): 6 sc into 2nd ch from hook, sl st to first sc, turn. 6 sts.

2nd round: Using A 1 ch (does NOT count as st), 2 sc into first sc, using B 1 sc into next sc, using A 2 sc into each of next 2 sc, 1 sc into next sc, 2 sc into last sc, sl st to first sc, turn. 10 sts.

3rd round: Using A 1 ch (does NOT count as st), 1 sc into each of first 6 sc, using B 1 sc into each of next 3 sc, using A 1 sc into last sc, sl st to first sc, turn.

4th round: Using A 1 ch (does NOT count

as st), 2 sc into first sc, using B 1 sc into each of next 3 sc, using A 2 sc into each of next 2 sc, 1 sc into each of next 3 sc, 2 sc into last sc, sl st to first sc, turn. 14 sts.

5th round: Using A 1 ch (does NOT count as st), 1 sc into each of first 8 sc, using B 1 sc into each of next 5 sc, using A 1 sc into last sc, sl st to first sc, turn.

6th round: Using A 1 ch (does NOT count as st), 1 sc into first sc, using B 1 sc into each of next 5 sc, using A 1 sc into each of last 8 sc, sl st to first sc, turn.

7th to 14th rounds: As 5th and 6th rounds 4 times.

15th round: Using A 1 ch (does NOT count as st), 1 sc into each of first 9 sc, using B 1 sc into each of next 3 sc, using A 1 sc into each of last 2 sc, sl st to first sc, turn.

16th round: Using A 1 ch (does NOT count as st), sc2tog over first 2 sc, using B 1 sc into each of next 3 sc, using A sc2tog over next 2 sc, 1 sc into each of last 7 sc, sl st to first sc, turn. 12 sts.

17th round: Using A 1 ch (does NOT count as st), sc2tog over first 2 sc, 1 sc into each of next 3 sc, sc2tog over next 2 sc, 1 sc into next sc, using B 1 sc into each of next 3 sc, using A 1 sc into last sc, sl st to first sc, turn.

18th round: Using A 1 ch (does NOT count as st), 1 sc into first sc, using B 1 sc into each of next 3 sc, using A 1 sc into each of last 6 sc, sl st to first sc, turn.

19th round: Using A 1 ch (does NOT count as st), 1 sc into each of first 6 sc, using B 1 sc into each of next 3 sc, using A 1 sc into last sc, sl st to first sc, turn.

20th and 21st rounds: As 18th and 19th

rounds.

22nd round: As 18th round.

Fasten off.

Press Ear flat, then make a pleat at base, with section in B inside pleat. Using photograph as a guide, sew Ears to top of Head.

Tail

With E4 (3.50 mm) hook and A, make 2 ch.

1st round (RS): 5 sc into 2nd ch from hook, sl st to first sc, turn. 5 sts.

2nd round: 1 ch (does NOT count as st), 2 sc into each sc to end, sl st to first sc, turn. 10 sts.

3rd round: 1 ch (does NOT count as st), (1 sc into next sc, 2 sc into next sc) 5 times, sl st to first sc, turn. 15 sts.

4th round: 1 ch (does NOT count as st), 1 sc into each sc to end, sl st to first sc, turn.

5th and 6th rounds: As 4th round.

7th round: 1 ch (does NOT count as st), (1 sc into next sc, sc2tog over next 2 sc) 5 times, sl st to first sc.

Fasten off.

Insert a little toy filling into Tail, then sew to back of Body just above Base.

Finishing

Using photograph as a guide, embroider french knot eyes using oddment of blue yarn. Using B, embroider satin stitch triangle for nose, then back stitch lines below nose to form mouth.

Hooded jacket

Keep your little one snug in this stylish hooded jacket! Made in a simple textured stitch using lofty cotton and microfiber yarn, this jacket is deceptively quick to stitch and sure to be a perennial favorite.

MEASUREMENTS

age	0–3	3–6	6–12	12–18	months
chest	16	18	20	22	in
	41	46	51	56	cm
actual chest	19¼	21½	24	26¾	in
	49	55	61	68	cm
length	9	10½	12¼	13¾	in
	23	27	31	35	cm
sleeve seam	5	6¼	7¾	10¼	in
	13	16	20	26	cm

MATERIALS

• 5 [5:6:6] x 50 g balls of Rowan All Seasons Cotton in Bleached 182
• Size H8 (5.00 mm) crochet hook
• 4 buttons

ABBREVIATIONS

• V-st—1 sc, 1 ch, and 1 sc
See also page 9.

GAUGE

19 stitches and 14 rows to 4 in (10 cm) measured over pattern using H8 (5.00 mm) hook.

Change hook size if necessary to obtain this gauge.

STITCH DIAGRAM

KEY

◯ ch
✛ sc

Body

(worked in one piece to armholes)

With H8 (5.00 mm) hook, make 102 [114:126:138] ch.

1st row (RS): 1 sc into 2nd ch from hook, skip 1 ch, *1 V-st into next ch**, skip 2 ch, rep from *to end, ending last rep at**

Now work in patt as follows:

2nd row: 1 ch (does NOT count as st), 1 sc into first sc, skip 1 sc, *1 V-st into next ch sp**, skip 2 sc, rep from * to end, ending last rep at **, skip 1 sc, 1 sc into last sc, turn.

This row forms patt.

Cont in patt until Body measures 4¾ [6:7:8¼] in (12 [15:18:21] cm), ending with WS facing for next row.

DIVIDE FOR ARMHOLES

Next row (WS): Patt until 7th [8th:9th:10th] V-st has been worked, skip 1 sc, 1 sc into next sc and turn, leaving rem sts unworked.

Work on this set of 23 [26:29:32] sts, 7 [8:9:10] patt reps only for left front. Cont straight until armhole measures 4¾ [4¾:5:5½] in (11 [12:13:14] cm), ending with RS facing for next row.

SHAPE SHOULDER

Fasten off, placing a marker 9 [11:13:15] sts in from armhole edge to denote inner edge of shoulder seam (14 [15:16:17] sts beyond marker at front opening edge).

SHAPE BACK

With WS facing, return to last complete row worked, skip next 10 sts, attach yarn to next sc, 1 ch (does NOT count as st), 1 sc into sc at base of 1 ch, skip 1 sc, 1 V-st into next ch sp, patt until 11 [13:15:17] V-sts in total have been worked, skip 1 sc, 1 sc into next sc and turn, leaving rem sts unworked.

Work on this set of 35 [41:47:53] sts, 11 [13:15:17] patt reps only for back. Cont straight until armhole measures 4¼ [4¾:5:5½] in (11 [12:13:14] cm), ending with RS facing for next row.

SHAPE SHOULDERS

Fasten off, placing markers either side of center 17 [19:21:23] sts to denote back neck.

SHAPE RIGHT FRONT

With WS facing, return to last complete row worked, skip next 10 sts, attach yarn to next sc, 1 ch (does NOT count as st), 1 sc into sc at base of 1 ch, skip 1 sc, 1 V-st into next ch sp, patt to end, turn.

23 [26:29:32] sts, 7 [8:9:10] patt reps. Complete to match left front. Do NOT fasten off at end of right front but slip working loop onto a safety pin and set aside this ball of yarn—it will be used later for Hood.

Sleeves

With H8 (5.00 mm) hook, make 24 [27:27:30] ch.

Work 1st and 2nd rows as given for Body. 23 [26:26:29] sts, 7 [8:8:9] patt reps.

3rd row: 1 ch (does NOT count as st), 2 sc into first sc, skip 1 sc, 1 V-st into next ch sp, patt until V-st has been worked into last ch sp, skip 1 sc, 2 sc into last sc, turn.

4th row: 1 ch (does NOT count as st), 2 sc into first sc, 1 sc into next sc, skip 1 sc, 1 V-st into next ch sp, patt until V-st has been worked into last ch sp, skip 1 sc, 1 sc into next sc, 2 sc into last sc, turn.

5th row: 1 ch (does NOT count as st), 1 sc into first sc, 1 V-st into next sc, skip 2 sc, 1 V-st into next ch sp, patt until V-st has been worked into last ch sp, skip 2 sc,

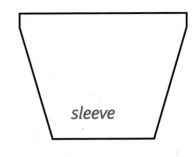

sleeve

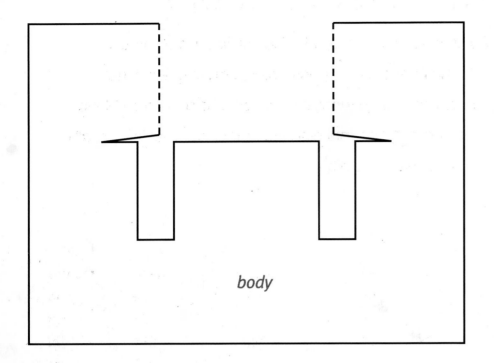

body

1 V-st into next sc, 1 sc into last sc, turn.
29 [32:32:35] sts, 9 [10:10:11] patt reps.
Work 1 [3:3:5] rows.
Rep last 4 [6:6:8] rows 1 [1:2:2] times more,
then 3rd to 5th rows again. 41 [44:50:53]
sts, 13 [14:16:17] patt reps.
Cont straight until Sleeve measures
5 [6¼:7¾:10¼] in (13 [16:20:26] cm).

SHAPE TOP

Place markers at both ends of last row to
denote top of sleeve seam.
Work a further 3 rows.
Fasten off.

Finishing

Join shoulder seams.

HOOD

Return to working loop left on safety pin
at end of right front and slip this loop
back onto H8 (5.00 mm) hook.
Working across sts of right front neck,
back neck, then left front neck, cont as
follows: 1 ch (does NOT count as st), 1 sc
into first sc, skip 1 sc, 1 V-st into next ch
sp, skip 2 sc, 1 V-st into next ch sp, (skip
1 st, 1 V-st into next st) 8 [9:10:11] times,
1 V-st into next ch sp (this is center back
neck ch sp), (1 V-st into next st, skip 1 st)
8 [9:10:11] times, 1 V-st into next ch sp,
skip 2 sc, 1 V-st into next ch sp, skip
1 sc, 1 sc into last sc, turn.
65 [71:77:83] sts, 21 [23:25:27] patt reps.
Cont in patt until Hood measures
7 [7½:8¼:8½] in (18 [19:21:22] cm).

Fold Hood in half, with RS innermost, and
join top seam of Hood by working a row
of sc through sts of both edges.
Fasten off.

Join sleeve seams below markers.
Matching sleeve markers to center of sts
skipped at underarm and center of last
row of Sleeve to shoulder seam, sew
Sleeves into armholes. Sew on buttons so
that front opening edges overlap by
1½ in (4 cm)—use ch sps of V-sts as
buttonholes, attach top button 2¼ in
(6 cm) below first row of Hood, lowest
button 2 in (5 cm) up from lower edge,
and rem 2 buttons evenly spaced
between.

Wrapover cardigan

Quick and easy to make, this little cardigan is worked in a simple mesh of doubles and chains, with single crochet edgings. The merino wool, microfiber, and cashmere blend yarn is ultra soft and machine washable too, making it really practical as well as pretty.

MEASUREMENTS

age	0–3	3–6	6–12	12–18	months
chest	16	18	20	22	in
	41	46	51	56	cm
actual chest	17¼	19¼	21½	23½	in
	44	49	55	60	cm
length	6½	8¼	9¾	11½	in
	17	21	25	29	cm
sleeve seam	5	6¼	7¾	9½	in
	13	16	20	24	cm

MATERIALS
• 2 [3:3:4] x 50 g balls of Rowan RYC Cashsoft Baby DK in Limone 802
• Size E4 (3.50 mm) crochet hook

ABBREVIATIONS
• **beg dec**—dec 2 sts (1 ch sp) over first 3 sts as follows: 4 ch (does NOT count as st), skip 2 sts at end of previous row, 1 dc into next dc—2 sts (1 ch sp) decreased
• **end dec**—dec 2 sts (1 ch sp) over last 3 sts of row as follows: yo and insert hook into next dc, yo and draw loop through, yo and draw through 2 loops, (yo) twice, skip 1 ch, insert hook into next st, yo and draw loop through, (yo and draw through 2 loops) twice, yo and draw through all 3 loops on hook—2 sts (1 ch sp) decreased
• **yo**—yarn over hook.
See also page 9.

GAUGE
22 sts and 10 rows to 4 in (10 cm) measured over pattern using E4 (3.50 mm) hook.
Change hook size if necessary to obtain this gauge.

Body

(worked in one piece to armholes)

With E4 (3.50 mm) hook, make 122 [140:154:168] ch.

1st row (RS): 1 sc into 2nd ch from hook, 1 sc into each ch to end, turn. 121 [139:153:167] sts.

2nd row: 4 ch (counts as first dc and 1 ch), skip first 2 sc, 1 dc into next sc, *1 ch, skip 1 sc, 1 dc into next sc, rep from * to end, turn. 60 [69:76:83] ch sps.

Now work in mesh patt as follows:

3rd row: 4 ch (counts as first dc and 1 ch), skip (dc at base of 4 ch and 1 ch), 1 dc into next dc, *1 ch, skip 1 ch, 1 dc into next dc, rep from * to end, working dc at end of last rep into 3rd of 4 ch at beg of previous row, turn.

This row forms mesh patt.

SHAPE FRONT SLOPES

Working all decreases as given in abbreviations, dec 2 sts at each end of next 4 [7:8:6] rows, then on 0 [0:1:3] foll alt rows. 105 [111:117:131] sts.

Work 0 [0:0:1] row. Body should measure 2¾ [4:5:6¼] in (7 [10:13:16] cm).

DIVIDE FOR ARMHOLES

Next row: Beg dec 1 [1:0:1] times, patt 21 [21:24:25] sts, end dec and turn, leaving rem sts unworked.

Work on this set of 23 [23:25:27] sts only for first front.

Dec 2 sts at armhole edge of next 1 [2:2:3] rows and at same time dec 2 sts at front

slope edge on next [next:next:2nd] and foll 0 [1:0:0] row. 19 [15:19:19] sts.

Dec 2 sts at front slope edge only on next [2nd:next:next] and foll 3 [0:0:0] rows, then on foll 1 [2:3:3] alt rows. 9 [9:11:11] sts.

Work 2 rows. Armhole should measure 4 [4¼:4¾:5] in (10 [11:12:13] cm).

SHAPE SHOULDER

Fasten off.

SHAPE BACK

Return to last complete row worked, skip next 3 sts, attach yarn to next dc and cont as follows:

Next row: Beg dec over st where yarn was attached and next 2 sts, patt 39 [45:51:57] sts, end dec and turn, leaving rem sts unworked.

Work on this set of 41 [47:53:59] sts only for back.

Dec 2 sts at each end of next 1 [2:2:3] rows.

37 [39:45:47] sts.

Work 7 [7:8:8] rows.

SHAPE BACK NECK AND SHOULDER

Next row: Patt 8 [8:10:10] sts, end dec and fasten off.

Return to last complete row worked before shaping back neck, skip next 15 [17:19:21] sts, attach yarn to next dc and cont as follows:

Next row: Beg dec over st where yarn was attached and next 2 sts, patt to end and fasten off.

STITCH DIAGRAM

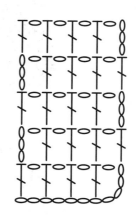

KEY

⬭ ch

🇹 dc

SHAPE SECOND FRONT

Return to last complete row worked before dividing for armholes, skip next 3 sts, attach yarn to next dc and cont as follows:

Next row: Beg dec over st where yarn was attached and next 2 sts, patt 21 [21:24:25] sts, end dec 1 [1:0:1] times, turn. 23 [23:25:27] sts.

Complete to match first front, reversing shapings.

Sleeves

With E4 (3.50 mm) hook, make 32 [32:36:36] ch.

Work 1st to 3rd rows as given for Body. 31 [31:35:35] sts, 15 [15:16:16] ch sps.

4th row: 5 ch (counts as first tr and 1 ch), 1 dc into dc at base of 5 ch—2 sts (1 ch sp) increased, patt to last st, (1 dc, 1 ch and 1 tr) into last st—2 sts (1 ch sp) increased, turn. 35 [35:37:37] sts.

Working all increases as set by last 2 rows, inc 2 sts at each end of 3rd [3rd:4th:4th]

Finishing

Join shoulder seams. Join sleeve seams. Insert sleeves into armholes, matching center of last row of sleeve to shoulder seam and top of sleeve seam to center of sts skipped at underarm.

NECK AND FRONT EDGING AND TIES

With RS facing and using E4 (3.50 mm) hook, attach yarn at end of foundation ch edge of Body at base of right front opening edge, 1 ch (does NOT count as st), work in sc up row-end edges to start of front slope shaping, *118 [127:137:146] ch, 1 sc into 2nd ch from hook, 1 sc into each ch back to start of front slope shaping*—this forms first tie, work in sc up right front slope, around back neck, then down left front slope to start of front slope shaping, rep from * to * again to form second tie, then work in sc down remainder of left front opening edge to foundation ch edge.

Fasten off.

and 1 [2:2:3] foll 3rd [3rd:4th:4th] rows. 43 [47:51:55] sts.

Work 3 [3:4:4] rows. (Sleeve should measure 5 [6¼:7¾:9½] in, 13 [16:20:24] cm.)

SHAPE TOP

Next row: Sl st across and into 3rd st, beg dec (4 sts in total decreased at this end of row), patt to last 5 sts, end dec and turn (4 sts in total decreased at this end of row). 35 [39:43:47] sts.

Dec 2 sts at each end of next 4 [5:6:7] rows. 19 sts.

Fasten off.

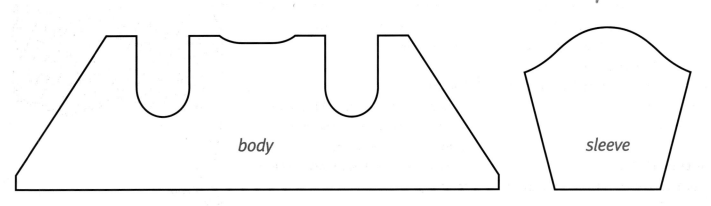

body

sleeve

Chevron tunic dress

Make your little one stand out in the crowd in this pretty little tunic dress! Bold stripes of color are worked in a chevron pattern made up of doubles for the skirt and sleeves, with narrower stripes of single crochet Finishing the circular yoke.

MEASUREMENTS

age	0–3	3–6	6–12	12–18	months
chest	16	18	20	22	in
	41	46	51	56	cm
actual size (at underarm)	17¼	20	22½	25	in
	44	51	58	64	cm
length (from upper edge)	10¼	12½	15	17¾	in
	26	32	38	45	cm
sleeve seam	5	6¼	8¼	10½	in
	13	16	21	27	cm

MATERIALS

• Rowan Pure Wool DK (50 g balls):
1 [2:2:2] balls in A (Dahlia 042), 1 [2:2:2] balls in B (Hyacinth 026), and 1 [2:2:2] balls in C (Tea Rose 025)
• Sizes E4 (3.50 mm) and G6 (4.00 mm) crochet hooks
• 1 button

ABBREVIATIONS

• **dc2tog**—leaving last loop of each dc on hook work 1 dc into next st, skip next st, 1 dc into next st, yo and draw through all 3 loops—2 sts decreased.
See also page 9.

GAUGE

18 stitches and 20 rows to 4 in (10 cm) measured over single crochet fabric using G6 (4.00 mm) hook.
Change hook size if necessary to obtain this gauge.

STITCH DIAGRAM

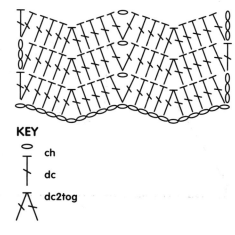

KEY

⊸ ch

† dc

⋏ dc2tog

Body

(worked in one piece to armholes)

With G6 (4.00 mm) hook and A, make 104 [124:144:164] ch.

1st row (RS): 1 dc into 4th ch from hook, *1 dc into each of next 3 ch, dc2tog over next 3 ch, 1 dc into each of next 3 ch**, (1 dc, 1 ch and 1 dc) into next ch, rep from * to end, ending last rep at **, 2 dc into last ch, turn. 10 [12:14:16] patt reps.

2nd row: 3 ch (counts as first dc), 1 dc into dc at base of 3 ch, *1 dc into each of next 3 dc, dc2tog over next 3 sts, 1 dc into each of next 3 dc**, (1 dc, 1 ch and 1 dc) into next ch sp, rep from * to end, ending last rep at **, 2 dc into top of 3 ch at beg of previous row, turn.

Last row forms chevron patt.

Joining in colors as required, now work in chevron patt in stripes as follows:

Using B, work 2 rows.

Using C, work 2 rows.

Using A, work 2 rows.

Last 6 rows form stripe sequence.

Work in chevron patt in stripe sequence as set for a further 5 [9:13:17] rows, ending after one row using A [C:B:A].

Next row (WS): Using same color as for previous row: 1 ch (does NOT count as st), 1 sc into first st, *skip 1 dc, 1 sc into next dc, 1 hdc into next dc, 1 dc into next dc, 1 tr into next dc2tog, 1 dc into next dc, 1 hdc into next dc, 1 sc into next dc, skip 1 dc**, 1 sc into next ch sp, rep from * to end, ending last rep at **, 1 sc into top of 3 ch at beg of previous row, turn. 81 [97:113:129] sts. Fasten off.

Sleeves

With G6 (4.00 mm) hook and C [A:A:A], make 54 [54:64:64] ch.

Work 1st and 2nd rows as given for Body. 5 [5:6:6] patt reps.

Working in chevron patt as now set and stripe sequence as given for Body, work a further 7 [9:13:17] rows, ending after one row using A [C:B:A].

Next row (WS): Using same color as for previous row: 1 ch (does NOT count as st), 1 sc into first st, *skip 1 dc, 1 sc into next dc, 1 hdc into next dc, 1 dc into next dc, 1 tr into next dc2tog, 1 dc into next dc, 1 hdc into next dc, 1 sc into next dc, skip 1 dc**, 1 sc into next ch sp, rep from * to end, ending last rep at **, 1 sc into top of 3 ch at beg of previous row, turn. 41 [41:49:49] sts. Fasten off.

Yoke

Using G6 (4.00 mm) hook and B [A:C:B], rejoin yarn to last st of last row of Body and join Body and Sleeves as follows:

1st row (RS): 1 ch (does NOT count as st), 1 sc into first st, 1 sc into each of next 8 [4:3:2] sts, sc2tog over next 2 sts, (1 sc into each of next 0 [10:7:6] sts, sc2tog over next 2 sc) 0 [1:2:3] times, 1 sc into each of next 9 [5:4:3] sts, now work across 41 [41:49:49] sts of first Sleeve as follows: 1 sc into each of first 4 [41:5:49] sts, (sc2tog over next 2 sts, 1 sc into each of next 8 [0:10:0] sts) 3 [0:3:0] times, (sc2tog over next 2 sts) 1 [0:1:0] times, 1 sc into each of last 5 [0:6:0] sts, now work across next 41 [49:57:65] sts of Body as follows: 1 sc into each of next 5 [3:3:3] sts, sc2tog over next 2 sts, (1 sc into each of next 12 [8:6:5] sts, sc2tog over next 2 sts) 2 [4:6:8] times, 1 sc into each of next 6 [4:4:4] sts, now work across 41 [41:49:49] sts of second Sleeve as follows: 1 sc into each of first 5 [41:6:49] sts, (sc2tog over next 2 sts, 1 sc into each of next 8 [0:10:0] sts) 3 [0:3:0] times, (sc2tog over next 2 sts) 1 [0:1:0] times, 1 sc into each of last 4 [0:5:0] sts, now work across rem 20 [24:28:32] sts of Body as follows: 1 sc into each of first 9 [5:4:3] sts, sc2tog over next 2 sts, (1 sc into each of next 0 [10:7:6] sts, sc2tog over next 2 sc) 0 [1:2:3] times, 1 sc into each of next 9 [5:4:3] sts, turn. 150 [170:190:210] sts.

Keeping stripe sequence correct as set by Body and Sleeves, cont as follows:

2nd row: 1 ch (does NOT count as st), 1 sc into each st to end, turn.

3rd row: 1 ch (does NOT count as st), (1 sc into each of next 4 sc, sc2tog over next 2 sc, 1 sc into each of next 4 sc) 15 [17:19:21] times, turn. 135 [153:171:189] sts.

4th and 5th rows: As 2nd row.

Change to E4 (3.50 mm) hook.

1st size only

6th row: 1 ch (does NOT count as st), (1 sc into each of next 3 sc, sc2tog over next 2 sc, 1 sc into each of next 4 sc) 15 times, turn. 120 sts.

7th and 8th rows: As 2nd row.

9th row: 1 ch (does NOT count as st), (1 sc into each of next 3 sc, sc2tog over next

2 sc, 1 sc into each of next 3 sc) 15 times, turn. 105 sts.

10th row: As 2nd row.

11th row: 1 ch (does NOT count as st), (1 sc into each of next 2 sc, sc2tog over next 2 sc, 1 sc into each of next 3 sc) 15 times, turn. 90 sts.

12th row: As 2nd row.

13th row: 1 ch (does NOT count as st), (1 sc into each of next 2 sc, sc2tog over next 2 sc, 1 sc into each of next 2 sc) 15 times, turn. 75 sts.

2nd size only

6th row: 1 ch (does NOT count as st), (1 sc into each of next 3 sc, sc2tog over next 2 sc, 1 sc into each of next 4 sc) 17 times, turn. 136 sts.

7th and 8th rows: As 2nd row.

9th row: 1 ch (does NOT count as st), (1 sc into each of next 3 sc, sc2tog over next 2 sc, 1 sc into each of next 3 sc) 17 times, turn. 119 sts.

10th row: As 2nd row.

11th row: 1 ch (does NOT count as st), (1 sc into each of next 16 sc, sc2tog over next 2 sc, 1 sc into each of next 3 sc) 5 times,

1 sc into each of last 14 sc, turn. 114 sts.

12th row: 1 ch (does NOT count as st), (1 sc into each of next 2 sc, sc2tog over next 2 sc, 1 sc into each of next 5 sc, sc2tog over next 2 sc, 1 sc into each of next 9 sc) 5 times, 1 sc into each of next 2 sc, sc2tog over next 2 sc, 1 sc into each of next 5 sc, sc2tog over next 2 sc, 1 sc into each of last 3 sc, turn. 102 sts.

13th row: 1 ch (does NOT count as st), (1 sc into each of next 14 sc, sc2tog over next 2 sc, 1 sc into each of next 2 sc) 5 times, 1 sc into each of last 12 sc, turn. 97 sts.

14th row: As 2nd row.

15th row: 1 ch (does NOT count as st), (1 sc into each of next 2 sc, sc2tog over next 2 sc, 1 sc into each of next 4 sc, sc2tog over next 2 sc, 1 sc into each of next 3 sc, sc2tog over next 2 sc, 1 sc into each of next 2 sc) 5 times, 1 sc into each of next 2 sc, sc2tog over next 2 sc, 1 sc into each of next 4 sc, sc2tog over next 2 sc, 1 sc into each of last 2 sc, turn. 80 sts.

3rd size only

6th row: 1 ch (does NOT count as st), (1 sc into each of next 12 sc, sc2tog over next 2 sc, 1 sc into each of next 4 sc) 9 times, 1 sc into each of last 9 sc, turn. 162 sts.

7th row: 1 ch (does NOT count as st), (1 sc into each of next 3 sc, sc2tog over next 2 sc, 1 sc into each of next 12 sc) 9 times, 1 sc into each of next 3 sc, sc2tog over next 2 sc, 1 sc into each of last 4 sc, turn. 152 sts.

8th row: As 2nd row.

9th row: 1 ch (does NOT count as st), (1 sc into each of next 11 sc, sc2tog over next 2 sc, 1 sc into each of next 3 sc) 9 times, 1 sc into each of last 8 sc, turn. 143 sts.

10th row: 1 ch (does NOT count as st), (1 sc into each of next 3 sc, sc2tog over next 2 sc, 1 sc into each of next 10 sc) 9 times, 1 sc into each of next 3 sc, sc2tog over next 2 sc, 1 sc into each of last 3 sc, turn. 133 sts.

11th row: As 2nd row.

12th row: 1 ch (does NOT count as st), (1 sc into each of next 9 sc, sc2tog over next 2 sc, 1 sc into each of next 3 sc) 9 times, 1 sc into each of last 7 sc, turn. 124 sts.

13th row: 1 ch (does NOT count as st), (1 sc into each of next 2 sc, sc2tog over next 2 sc, 1 sc into each of next 9 sc) 9 times, 1 sc into each of next 2 sc, sc2tog over next 2 sc, 1 sc into each of last 3 sc, turn. 114 sts.

14th row: As 2nd row.

15th row: 1 ch (does NOT count as st), (1 sc into each of next 8 sc, sc2tog over next 2 sc, 1 sc into each of next 2 sc) 9 times, 1 sc into each of last 6 sc, turn. 105 sts.

16th row: 1 ch (does NOT count as st), (1 sc into each of next 2 sc, sc2tog over next 2 sc, 1 sc into each of next 7 sc) 9 times, 1 sc into each of next 2 sc, sc2tog over next 2 sc, 1 sc into each of last 2 sc, turn. 95 sts.

17th row: 1 ch (does NOT count as st), (1 sc into each of next 6 sc, sc2tog over next 2 sc, 1 sc into each of next 2 sc) 9 times, 1 sc into each of last 5 sc, turn. 86 sts.

4th size only

6th row: 1 ch (does NOT count as st), (1 sc into each of next 3 sc, sc2tog over next 2 sc, 1 sc into each of next 16 sc, sc2tog over next 2 sc, 1 sc into each of next 4 sc) 7 times, turn. 175 sts.

7th row: 1 ch (does NOT count as st), (1 sc into each of next 11 sc, sc2tog over next 2 sc, 1 sc into each of next 12 sc) 7 times, turn. 168 sts.

8th row: As 2nd row.

9th row: 1 ch (does NOT count as st), (1 sc into each of next 3 sc, sc2tog over next 2 sc, 1 sc into each of next 14 sc, sc2tog over next 2 sc, 1 sc into each of next 3 sc) 7 times, turn. 154 sts.

10th row: As 2nd row.

11th row: 1 ch (does NOT count as st), (1 sc into each of next 10 sc, sc2tog over next 2 sc, 1 sc into each of next 10 sc) 7 times, turn. 147 sts.

12th row: 1 ch (does NOT count as st), (1 sc into each of next 2 sc, sc2tog over next 2 sc, 1 sc into each of next 12 sc, sc2tog over next 2 sc, 1 sc into each of next 3 sc) 7 times, turn. 133 sts.

13th and 14th rows: As 2nd row.

15th row: 1 ch (does NOT count as st), (1 sc into each of next 2 sc, sc2tog over next 2 sc, 1 sc into each of next 4 sc, sc2tog over next 2 sc, 1 sc into each of next 5 sc, sc2tog over next 2 sc, 1 sc into each of next 2 sc) 7 times, turn. 112 sts.

16th and 17th rows: As 2nd row.

18th row: 1 ch (does NOT count as st), (1 sc into next sc, sc2tog over next 2 sc, 1 sc into each of next 4 sc, sc2tog over next 2 sc, 1 sc into each of next 3 sc, sc2tog over next 2 sc, 1 sc into each of next 2 sc) 7 times, turn. 91 sts.

19th row: As 2nd row.

All sizes

Next row (WS): 1 ch (does NOT count as st), 1 sc into each st to end, 5 ch (to make button loop), sl st to last sc.
Fasten off.

Finishing

Join sleeve seams. Join center back seam, leaving seam open for 2¼ in (6 cm) at neck edge. Sew on button.

Puppy carriage string

Keep your little treasures amused while out in the carriage by entertaining them with these spirited puppies. Easily made in single crochet, their cute little ribbon bows match the ribbon they are suspended from. Make one on its own and use it to decorate a rattle.

MEASUREMENTS
Each Puppy stands approx 4 in (10 cm) tall, and measures approx 4¼ in (11 cm) from nose to tail.

MATERIALS
• 1 x 50 g ball of Rowan Pure Wool DK in each of cream (Enamel 013), beige (Hay 014), light brown (Hessian 016) and dark brown (Earth 018)
• Size E4 (3.50 mm) crochet hook
• Washable toy filling
• 47¼ in (120 cm) of ³⁄₈ in (1 cm)-wide plaid ribbon
• 47¼ in (120 cm) of 1 in (2.5 cm)-wide plaid ribbon

ABBREVIATIONS
See page 9.

GAUGE
19 stitches and 20 rows to 4 in (10 cm) measured over single crochet fabric using E4 (3.50 mm) hook.
Change hook size if necessary to obtain this gauge.

STITCH DIAGRAM

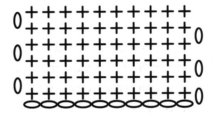

KEY

⊖ ch
+ sc

Legs *(make four)*

With E4 (3.50 mm) hook and cream, make 3 ch.

1st round (RS): 2 sc into 2nd ch from hook, 4 sc into last ch, working back along other side of ch: 2 sc into same ch as first 2 sc, sl st to first sc, turn. 8 sts.

2nd round: 1 ch (does NOT count as st), 2 sc into first sc, 1 sc into each of next 2 sc, 2 sc into each of next 2 sc, 1 sc into each of next 2 sc, 2 sc into last sc, sl st to first sc, turn. 12 sts.

Break off cream and join in beige.

3rd round: 1 ch (does NOT count as st), 1 sc into each sc to end, sl st to first sc, turn.

4th round: 1 ch (does NOT count as st), 1 sc into each of first 4 sc, (sc2tog over next 2 sc) twice, 1 sc into each of last 4 sc, sl st to first sc, turn. 10 sts.

5th round: As 3rd round.

6th round: 1 ch (does NOT count as st), sc2tog over first 2 sc, 1 sc into each of next 6 sc, sc2tog over last 2 sc, sl st to first sc, turn. 8 sts.

7th round: As 3rd round. Fasten off. Insert a tiny amount of toy filling and fold top of Leg flat—start and ends of rounds form back fold edge.

Tail

With E4 (3.50 mm) hook and light brown, make 2 ch.

1st round (RS): 4 sc into 2nd ch from hook, sl st to first sc, turn. 4 sts.

2nd round: 1 ch (does NOT count as st), 1 sc into each of sc to end, sl st to first sc, turn.

3rd round: As 2nd round.

Fasten off. Fold Tail flat.

Body

BASE

With E4 (3.50 mm) hook and beige, make 5 ch.

1st row (RS): 1 sc into 2nd ch from hook, 1 sc into each ch to end, turn. 4 sts.

2nd row: 1 ch (does NOT count as st), 2 sc into first sc, 1 sc into each of next 2 sc, 2 sc into last sc, turn. 6 sts.

3rd row: 1 ch (does NOT count as st), 2 sc into first sc, 1 sc into each of next 4 sc, 2 sc into last sc, turn. 8 sts.

4th row: 1 ch (does NOT count as st), 1 sc into each sc to end, turn.

5th to 8th rows: As 4th row.

9th row: 1 ch (does NOT count as st), sc2tog over first 2 sc, 1 sc into each of next 4 sc, sc2tog over last 2 sc, turn. 6 sts.

10th row: As 4th row.

Fasten off.

Foundation ch edge of Base is back edge.

BODY

With RS facing, E4 (3.50 mm) hook and beige, attach yarn at center of last row of Base and work around entire outer edge of Base as follows:

1st round: 1 ch (does NOT count as st), work 1 sc each of last 3 sts of "next" row of Base, then working 1 sc into each row-end edge and holding Legs against RS of Base, work 1 sc into each of first 4 row-end edges enclosing top folded edge of first Leg in sts (make sure Foot points towards front!), 1 sc into each of next 2 row-end edges, work 1 sc into each of next 4 row-end edges enclosing top folded edge of second Leg in sts, work 1 sc into each foundation ch of Base (4 sts), then working 1 sc into each row-end edge and holding Legs against RS of Base, work 1 sc into each of first 4 row-end edges enclosing top folded edge of third Leg in sts, 1 sc into each of next 2 row-end edges, work 1 sc into each of last 4 row-end edges enclosing top folded edge of fourth Leg in sts, then work 1 sc each of first

3 sts of "next" row of Base, sl st to first sc, turn. 30 sts.

2nd round (WS): 1 ch (does NOT count as st), 2 sc into first sc, 1 sc into each of next 13 sc, 2 sc into each of next 2 sc, 1 sc into each of next 13 sc, 2 sc into last sc, sl st to first sc, turn. 34 sts.

3rd round: 1 ch (does NOT count as st), 1 sc into each sc to end, sl st to first sc, turn.

4th and 5th rounds: As 3rd round.

SHAPE OPENING FOR HEAD

Now working in rows, not rounds, cont as follows:

6th row: 1 ch (does NOT count as st), sc2tog over first 2 sc, 1 sc into each sc to last 2 sc, sc2tog over last 2 sc, turn.

7th row: As 6th row. 30 sts.

8th row: 1 ch (does NOT count as st), sc2tog over first 2 sc, 1 sc into each of next 11 sc, (sc2tog over next 2 sc) twice, 1 sc into each of next 11 sc, sc2tog over last 2 sc, turn. 26 sts.

9th row: 1 ch (does NOT count as st), sc2tog over first 2 sc, 1 sc into each of next 9 sc, (sc2tog over next 2 sc) twice, 1 sc into each of next 9 sc, sc2tog over last 2 sc, turn. 22 sts.

Fasten off. Fold Body in half and join top of last row to form top seam, enclosing end of Tail in seam near fold. Insert toy filling so Body is firmly filled.

Ears (make two)

With E4 (3.50 mm) hook and light brown, make 4 ch.

1st round (RS): 1 sc into 2nd ch from hook, 1 sc into each of next 2 ch, working back along other side of foundation ch: 1 sc into each of next 3 ch, sl st to first sc, turn. 6 sts.

2nd round: 1 ch (does NOT count as st), 2 sc into first sc, 1 sc into next sc, 2 sc into each of next 2 sc, 1 sc into next sc, 2 sc into last sc, sl st to first sc, turn. 10 sts.

3rd round: 1 ch (does NOT count as st), 1 sc into each sc to end, sl st to first sc, turn.

4th and 5th rounds: As 3rd round.

6th round: 1 ch (does NOT count as st), sc2tog over first 2 sc, 1 sc into next sc, (sc2tog over next 2 sc) twice, 1 sc into next sc, sc2tog over last 2 sc, sl st to first sc, turn. 6 sts.

7th round: As 3rd round.

8th round: 1 ch (does NOT count as st), 1 sc into each of first 2 sc, sc2tog over next 2 sc, 1 sc into each of last 2 sc, sl st to first sc, turn. 5 sts.

9th round: As 3rd round.

Fasten off.

Fold Ear flat so that it forms a 6 shape—straighter edge is back edge.

Head

With E4 (3.50 mm) hook and beige, make 14 ch and join with a sl st to form a ring.

1st round (RS): 1 ch (does NOT count as st), 1 sc into each ch to end, sl st to first sc, turn. 14 sts.

2nd round: 1 ch (does NOT count as st), 2 sc into first sc, 1 sc into each of next 5 sc, 2 sc into each of next 2 sc, 1 sc into each of next 5 sc, 2 sc into last sc, sl st to first sc, turn.

18 sts.

3rd round: 1 ch (does NOT count as st),
1 sc into each sc to end, sl st to first sc,
turn.

4th and 5th rounds: As 3rd round.

6th round: 1 ch (does NOT count as st),
sc2tog over first 2 sc, 1 sc into each of next
5 sc, (sc2tog over next 2 sc) twice,
1 sc into each of next 5 sc, sc2tog over last
2 sc, sl st to first sc, turn. 14 sts.

7th round: 1 ch (does NOT count as st),
sc2tog over first 2 sc, 1 sc into each of next
3 sc, (sc2tog over next 2 sc) twice,
1 sc into each of next 3 sc, sc2tog over last
2 sc, sl st to first sc, turn. 10 sts.
Fasten off.

Sew top seam of Head by joining top of
last round and enclosing Ears in seam.
Insert toy filling so Head is quite firmly
filled. Sew foundation ch edge of Head to
opening in Body, adding a little extra filling
into neck section.

Muzzle

With E4 (3.50 mm) hook and cream, make
2 ch.

1st round (RS): 8 sc into 2nd ch from hook,
sl st to first sc, turn. 8 sts.

2nd round: 1 ch (does NOT count as st),
1 sc into first sc, 2 sc into each of next
2 sc, 1 sc into each of next 2 sc, 2 sc into
each of next 2 sc, 1 sc into last sc, sl st to
first sc, turn. 12 sts.

3rd round: 1 ch (does NOT count as st),
1 sc into first sc, (2 sc into next sc, 1 sc into

each of next 2 sc) 3 times, 2 sc into next
sc, 1 sc into last sc, sl st to first sc, turn.
16 sts.

4th round: 1 ch (does NOT count as st),
1 sc into each sc to end, sl st to first sc,
turn.

5th to 7th rounds: As 4th round.
Fasten off.

Insert toy filling so Muzzle is quite firmly
filled. Sew Muzzle to front of Head as in
photograph. Catch stitch Ears to sides of
Muzzle as in photograph.

Nose

With E4 (3.50 mm) hook and light brown,
make 2 ch.

1st round (RS): 6 sc into 2nd ch from hook,
sl st to first sc, turn. 6 sts.

2nd round: 1 ch (does NOT count as st),

(sc2tog over next 2 sc) 3 times, sl st to first
sc. 3 sts.
Fasten off.

Using photograph as a guide, sew Nose
to Muzzle.

Finishing

Using photograph as a guide and dark
brown yarn, embroider french knot eyes
and straight stitch mouth. Tie 12 in (30 cm)
length of narrow ribbon in a bow around
neck. Thread wider ribbon through center
top of body and tie in a knot.

Make four Basic Puppies—two puppies
using colors as given, and two puppies
using colors as follows: use beige instead
of cream, light brown instead of beige,
and dark brown instead of light brown.
Embroider eyes and mouths using
darkest shade used for each puppy.

Tie a knot in wider ribbon approx
12 in (30 cm) from one end. Using
photograph as a guide, thread ribbon
through top of first puppy just behind its
neck, and tie ribbon in a knot again to
secure this puppy in place. Knot ribbon
again approx 2¼ in (6 cm) from last
puppy, thread on next puppy and knot
ribbon again to secure this puppy in
place. Cont in this way until all 4 puppies
are knotted onto ribbon, then trim free
end of ribbon to match first end.

For a simpler, quicker project, just make
one puppy and tie to a length of wide
ribbon—this can then be attached to a
rattle, highchair, or favorite toy.

All-in-one

Keep your cherub warm in this practical all-in-one. Simply made in single crochet, the tweedy yarn creates the color interest. It fastens with a practical zipper opening and the doubled cuffs at the wrist and ankles will keep out the drafts.

MEASUREMENTS

age	0–3	3–6	6–12	12–18	months
chest	16	18	20	22	in
	41	46	51	56	cm
actual chest (at underarm)	19¼	22	24½	27	in
	49	56	62	69	cm
length (from shoulder to ankle)	18½	20	22½	24¾	in
	47	51	57	63	cm
sleeve seam	4¾	6	7½	9	in
	12	15	19	23	cm

MATERIALS

• 6 [6:7:8] x 50 g balls of Twilley's Freedom Spirit in Fire 402
• Sizes E4 (3.50 mm) and G6 (4.00 mm) crochet hooks
• Zipper to fit front opening

ABBREVIATIONS

See page 9.

GAUGE

18 stitches and 21 rows to 4 in (10 cm) measured over single crochet fabric using G6 (4.00 mm) hook. Change hook size if necessary to obtain this gauge.

STITCH DIAGRAM

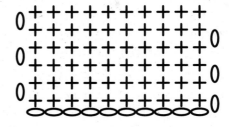

KEY

○ ch
+ sc

Body

FIRST LEG

With E4 (3.50 mm) hook, make 26 [30:34:38] ch and join with a sl st to form a ring.

1st round (RS): 1 ch (does NOT count as st), 1 sc into each ch to end, sl st to first sc, turn. 26 [30:34:38] sts.

2nd round: 1 ch (does NOT count as st), 1 sc into each sc to end, sl st to first sc, turn.

Last round forms sc fabric worked in rounds.

Work in sc fabric for a further 4 rounds.

Place marker at end of last round.

Work a further 6 rounds.

Change to G6 (4.00 mm) hook.

13th round (RS): 1 ch (does NOT count as st), (1 sc into first sc) 0 [1:1:1] times, 2 sc into each of next 2 sc, (1 sc into next sc, 2 sc into each of next 2 sc) 8 [9:10:11] times, 1 sc into each of last 0 [0:1:2] sc, sl st to first sc, turn. 44 [50:56:62] sts.

Cont in sc fabric until First Leg measures 4 [4¾:5½:6¼] in (10 [12:14:16] cm) from marked round, ending after a WS round.

Next round (RS): 1 ch (does NOT count as st), 2 sc into first sc, 1 sc into each sc to last sc, 2 sc into last sc, sl st to first sc, turn. 46 [52:58:64] sts.

Work 1 round.

Next round: 1 ch (does NOT count as st), 2 sc into first sc, 1 sc into each sc to last sc, 2 sc into last sc, sl st to first sc, turn. 48 [54:60:66] sts.

Rep last round 3 times more, ending after a WS round. 54 [60:66:72] sts.**

Break yarn.

SECOND LEG

Work as given for First Leg to **.

JOIN LEGS

Next round (RS): 1 ch (does NOT count as st), 1 sc into each sc of Second Leg, then 1 sc into each sc of First Leg, sl st to first sc, turn. 108 [120:132:144] sts.

Work 3 [5:3:7] rounds.

Next round: 1 ch (does NOT count as st), 1 sc into each of first 25 [28:31:34] sc, (sc2tog over next 2 sc) twice, 1 sc into each of next 50 [56:62:68] sc, (sc2tog over next 2 sc) twice, 1 sc into each of last 25 [28:31:34] sc, sl st to first sc, turn. 104 [116:128:140] sts.

Work 4 [6:9:9] rounds.

3rd and 4th sizes only

Next round: 1 ch (does NOT count as st), 1 sc into each of first [30:33] sc, (sc2tog over next 2 sc) twice, 1 sc into each of next [60:66] sc, (sc2tog over next 2 sc) twice, 1 sc into each of last [30:33] sc, sl st to first sc, turn. [124:136] sts.

Work [1:0] rounds.

All sizes

Next row: 1 ch (does NOT count as st), 1 sc into each sc to end, turn.

Last row forms sc fabric worked in rows.

Work in sc fabric for a further 2 [0:7:8] rows.

Next row: 1 ch (does NOT count as st), 1 sc into each of first 24 [27:29:32] sc, (sc2tog over next 2 sc) twice, 1 sc into each of next 48 [54:58:64] sc, (sc2tog over next 2 sc) twice, 1 sc into each of last 24 [27:29:32] sc, turn. 100 [112:120:132] sts.

Work 7 [7:9:9] rows.

Next row: 1 ch (does NOT count as st), 1 sc into each of first 23 [26:28:31] sc, (sc2tog over next 2 sc) twice, 1 sc into each of next 46 [52:56:62] sc, (sc2tog over next 2 sc) twice, 1 sc into each of last 23 [26:28:31] sc, turn. 96 [108:116:128] sts.

Work 7 [7:9:9] rows.

Next row: 1 ch (does NOT count as st), 1 sc into each of first 22 [25:27:30] sc, (sc2tog over next 2 sc) twice, 1 sc into each of next 44 [50:54:60] sc, (sc2tog over next 2 sc) twice, 1 sc into each of last 22 [25:27:30] sc, turn. 92 [104:112:124] sts.

1st and 2nd sizes only

Work 7 rows.

Next row: 1 ch (does NOT count as st), 1 sc into each of first 21 [24] sc, (sc2tog over next 2 sc) twice, 1 sc into each of next 42 [48] sc, (sc2tog over next 2 sc) twice, 1 sc into each of last 21 [24] sc, turn. 88 [100] sts.

All sizes

Cont straight until work measures 9½ [9¾:11:12¼] in (24 [25:28:31] cm) from leg joining row, ending after a WS row.

SHAPE BACK

Slip working loop onto a safety pin and set aside ball of yarn in use.

With RS facing, skip first 25 [28:31:34] sts of next row, rejoin new ball of yarn to next st and cont as follows:

Next row: 1 ch (does NOT count as st), 1 sc into sc where yarn was rejoined, 1 sc into each of next 37 [43:49:55] sts and turn. Work on this set of 38 [44:50:56] sts only for back.

Dec 1 st (by working sc2tog over edge 2 sts) at each end of next 3 rows, then on foll 2 [3:4:5] alt rows. 28 [32:36:40] sts.

Cont straight until armhole measures 3½ [4:4¼:4¾] in (9 [10:11:12] cm), ending after a WS row.

SHAPE BACK NECK

Next row (RS): 1 ch (does NOT count as st), 1 sc into each of first 7 [8:9:10] sc and turn, leaving rem sts unworked.
Dec 1 st at beg of next row. 6 [7:8:9] sts.

SHAPE SHOULDER

Fasten off.

Return to last complete row worked before shaping back neck, skip next 14 [16:18:20] sts, rejoin yarn to next st and work as follows:

Next row (RS): 1 ch (does NOT count as st), 1 sc into sc where yarn was rejoined, 1 sc into each of last 6 [7:8:9] sc, turn.
Dec 1 st at end of next row. 6 [7:8:9] sts.

SHAPE SHOULDER

Fasten off.

SHAPE RIGHT FRONT

Return to st left on safety pin. Slip this st back onto hook and cont as follows:
Next row (RS): 1 ch (does NOT count as st),

1 sc into each of first 19 [22:25:28] sc and turn. (There should be 6 sc left unworked between last st of right front and first st of back.)

Dec 1 st at armhole edge of next 3 rows, then on foll 2 [3:4:5] alt rows.
14 [16:18:20] sts.

Cont straight until 8 [8:10:10] rows less have been worked than on back to shoulder fasten-off point, ending after a WS row.

SHAPE NECK

Next row (RS): Sl st across and into 4th [5th:5th:6th] sc, 1 ch (does NOT count as st), 1 sc into same place as last sl st— 3 [4:4:5] sts decreased, 1 sc into each sc to end, turn. 11 [12:14:15] sts.
Dec 1 st at neck edge of next 4 rows, then on foll 1 [1:2:2] alt rows. 6 [7:8:9] sts.
Work 1 row.

SHAPE SHOULDER

Fasten off.

SHAPE LEFT FRONT

Return to last complete row worked before shaping back, skip next 6 sc, re-join yarn to next sc, 1 ch (does NOT count as st), 1 sc into same place as where yarn was rejoined, 1 sc into each sc to end, turn. 19 [22:25:28] sts.

Dec 1 st at armhole edge of next 3 rows, then on foll 2 [3:4:5] alt rows.
14 [16:18:20] sts.

Cont straight until 8 [8:10:10] rows less have been worked than on back to shoulder fasten-off point, ending after a WS row.

SHAPE NECK

Next row (RS): 1 ch (does NOT count as st), 1 sc into each of first 11 [12:14:15] sc and turn, leaving rem sts unworked—3 [4:4:5] sts decreased. 11 [12:14:15] sts.
Dec 1 st at neck edge of next 4 rows, then on foll 1 [1:2:2] alt rows. 6 [7:8:9] sts.
Work 1 row.

SHAPE SHOULDER

Fasten off.

Sleeves

With E4 (3.50 mm) hook, make 22 [24:26:28] ch and join with a sl st to form a ring.
1st round (RS): 1 ch (does NOT count as st), 1 sc into each ch to end, sl st to first sc, turn. 22 [24:26:28] sts.
Work in rounds of sc fabric for a further 5 rounds.
Place marker at end of last round.
Work a further 6 rounds.
Change to G6 (4.00 mm) hook.
13th round: 1 ch (does NOT count as st), 1 sc into each of first 4 [3:3:2] sc, 2 sc into each of next 2 sc, (1 sc into next sc, 2 sc into each of next 2 sc) 4 [5:6:7] times, 1 sc into each of last 4 [4:3:3] sc, sl st to first sc, turn. 32 [36:40:44] sts.
Cont in sc fabric until Sleeve measures 4¾ [6:7½:9] in (12 [15:19:23] cm) from marked round, ending after a WS round and remembering to turn at end of last round.

SHAPE TOP

Working all shaping as given for Body and

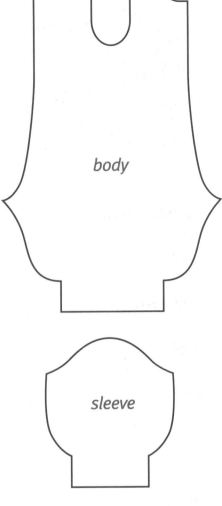

body

sleeve

now working in rows, not rounds, dec 3 sts at each end of next row. 26 [30:34:38] sts. Dec 1 st at each end of next 9 [11:13:15] rows. 8 sts.

Fasten off.

Finishing

Join shoulder seams. Sew sleeves into armholes.

COLLAR

With RS facing and using E4 (3.50 mm) hook, attach yarn at top of right front opening edge, 1 ch (does NOT count as st), work 11 [12:14:15] sc up right side of neck, 16 [18:20:22] sc across back neck, then z11 [12:14:15] sc down left side of neck to top of left front opening edge, turn. 38 [42:48:52] sts.

Work in rows of sc fabric for 13 rows, ending after a WS row.
Fasten off.

Sew zipper into front opening, positioning top of zipper teeth approx 4 rows up from first row of collar. Fold collar in half to inside and slip stitch in place. Fold first 6 rounds of legs and sleeves to inside and slip stitch in place.

Hooded sweater

This little sweater is given extra impact by the use of a stunning hand-dyed yarn. The tweedy textures and bright colors of the yarn turn a simple stitch pattern into something really special. And, as the yarn is quite thick, it can be made really quickly too!

MEASUREMENTS

age	0–3	3–6	6–12	12–18	months
chest	16	18	20	22	in
	41	46	51	56	cm
actual chest	19	21½	24½	26¾	in
	48	55	62	68	cm
length	9	10½	12¼	13¾	in
	23	27	31	35	cm
sleeve seam	5	6¼	7¾	10¼	in
	13	16	20	26	cm

MATERIALS

• 3 [3:3:4] x 100 g hanks of Colinette Prism in Neptune 139
• Size 19 (5.50 mm) crochet hook

ABBREVIATIONS

See page 9.

GAUGE

12 stitches and 9 rows to 4 in (10 cm) measured over pattern using 19 (5.50 mm) hook. Change hook size if necessary to obtain this gauge.

STITCH DIAGRAM

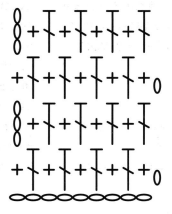

KEY

○ ch
+ sc
┼ dc

Back

With I9 (5.50 mm) hook, make
30 [34:38:42] ch.

Foundation row (RS): 1 sc into 2nd ch
from hook, *1 dc into next ch, 1 sc into
next ch, rep from * to end, turn.
29 [33:37:41] sts.

Now work in patt as follows:

1st row: 3 ch (counts as first dc), skip sc
at base of 3 ch, *1 sc into next dc, 1 dc
into next sc, rep from * to end, turn.

2nd row: 1 ch (does NOT count as st),
1 sc into dc at base of 1 ch, *1 dc into next
sc, 1 sc into next dc, rep from * to end,
working sc at end of last rep into top of
3 ch at beg of previous row, turn.

Last 2 rows form patt.

Cont in patt until Back measures approx
5 [6¼:7½:8½] in (13 [16:19:22] cm),
ending with RS facing for next row.

SHAPE ARMHOLES

Next row (RS): Sl st across and into 3rd
st, 1 ch (does NOT count as st), 1 sc into
dc at base of 1 ch—2 sts decreased, *1
dc into next sc, 1 sc into next dc, rep from
* to last 2 sts and turn, leaving rem 2 sts
unworked—2 sts decreased.
25 [29:33:37] sts.**

Cont straight until armhole measures
4 [4¼:4¾:5] in (10 [11:12:13] cm), ending
with RS facing for next row.

SHAPE SHOULDERS

Fasten off, placing markers either side of
center 11 [11:13:15] sts to denote back neck.

Front

Work as given for Back to **.
Work 1 row, ending with RS facing for
next row.

DIVIDE FOR FRONT OPENING

Next row (RS): Patt 12 [14:16:18] sts and
turn, leaving rem sts unworked.
Cont in patt on these sts until Front
matches Back to fasten-off point.
Fasten off, placing marker 5 [5:6:7] sts in
from front opening edge to denote front
neck shoulder point.

With RS facing, return to last complete row
worked, skip next st, attach yarn to next
st, make turning ch, patt to end, turn.
12 [14:16:18] sts.
Complete to match first side. Do NOT
fasten off but slip working loop onto a
safety pin and set aside this ball of yarn—
it will be used later for Hood.

Sleeves

With I9 (5.50 mm) hook, make
18 [20:22:24] ch.
Work foundation row and 1st patt row as
given for Back. 17 [19:21:23] sts.

Next row: 3 ch (counts as 1 dc), 1 sc into
dc at base of 3 ch—1 st increased, *1 dc
into next sc, 1 sc into next dc, rep from *
to end, working sc at end of last rep into
top of 3 ch at beg of previous row, 1 dc
into same place as last sc—1 st
increased, turn.

Working all increases in this way (by
working 2 sts into first and last st of row)
and keeping patt correct, cont in patt, inc
1 st at each end of 2nd [3rd:3rd:4th] and
every foll alt [3rd:3rd:4th] row until there
are 25 [27:31:33] sts.

Cont straight until Sleeve measures
5 [6¼:7¾:10¼] in (13 [16:20:26] cm),
ending with RS facing for next row.

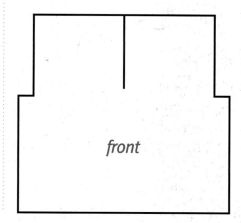

front

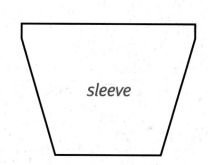

sleeve

edge, keeping patt correct as set by these 2 sts now work 2 sts into each of next 8 [8:10:12] sts, patt next st (this is center back neck st), work 2 sts into each of next 8 [8:10:12] sts, then patt rem 2 sts at top of left front opening edge, turn. 37 [37:45:53] sts. Cont in patt until Hood measures 5 [5½:6:6¼] in (13 [14:15:16] cm), ending with RS facing for next row.

Next row: Make turning ch and patt first 17 [17:21:25] sts, skip next st, 1 dc into next st (this is center st of row), skip next st, patt to end, turn.

Next row: Make turning ch and patt to within 1 st of center dc, skip next st, 1 dc into center dc, skip next st, patt to end, turn. Rep last row twice more. 29 [29:37:45] sts. Fold Hood in half, with RS innermost, and join top seam of Hood by working a row of sc through sts of both edges.
Fasten off.

Matching sleeve markers to top of side seam and center of last row of Sleeve to shoulder seam, sew Sleeves into armholes. Join side and sleeve seams.

FRONT OPENING AND HOOD EDGING

With RS facing and using 19 (5.50 mm) hook, attach yarn at base of right front opening edge, 1 ch (does NOT count as st), work in sc evenly up right side of opening, then up right side of Hood, down left side of Hood, then down left front opening edge to base of opening, sl st to first sc.
Fasten off.

SHAPE TOP

Place markers at both ends of last row to denote top of sleeve seam.
Work a further 2 rows.
Fasten off.

Finishing

Join shoulder seams.

HOOD

Return to working loop left on safety pin at top of right front opening edge and slip this loop back onto 19 (5.50 mm) hook.
With RS facing and working across 5 [5:6:7] sts of right front neck, 11 [11:13:15] sts of back neck, and then 5 [5:6:7] sts of left front neck, cont as follows: make turning ch and patt first 2 sts at right front neck

vest and hat

A fluffy yarn and a bobbly stitch pattern are combined to create this little vest and hat set! Made using a soft cashmere blend yarn worked together with a mohair and silk yarn, it's a little touch of luxury for your baby.

MEASUREMENTS

age	0–3	3–6	6–12	12–18	months
VEST					
chest	16	18	20	22	in
	41	46	51	56	cm
actual size	19¼	21½	24	26¼	in
	49	55	61	67	cm
length	8½	9¾	11¼	13¼	in
	22	25	29	34	cm
HAT					
width around head	12¼	14	15¾	17¼	in
	31	36	40	44	cm

VEST MATERIALS

• 2 [2:3:3] x 50 g balls of Rowan RYC Cashsoft DK in M (Ballad Blue 508)
• 2 [3:3:4] x 25 g balls of Rowan Aura in C (Steel 758)

HAT MATERIALS

• 1 [1:1:1] x 50 g ball of Rowan RYC Cashsoft DK in M (Ballad Blue 508)

• 1 [1:1:1] x 25 g ball of Rowan Aura in C (Steel 758)

VEST AND HAT

• Sizes E4 (3.50 mm) and 7 (4.50 mm) crochet hooks
• 5 buttons for Vest

ABBREVIATIONS

See page 9.

GAUGE

13½ stitches and 12 rows to 4 in (10 cm) measured over pattern using one strand of M and one strand of C together and 7 (4.50 mm) hook.
Change hook size if necessary to obtain this gauge.

Pattern and shaping note

Pattern is basically a sc fabric with tiny "bobbles" created on WS rows by working a taller tr st. When shaping through patt, do NOT work these taller tr sts on edge sts of rows as this may distort the work. Simply work them as a sc.

Decreases

To dec 1 st at beg of row, beg row with: "1 ch (does NOT count as st), sc2tog over first 2 sts—1 st decreased."

To dec 1 st at end of row, patt to last 2 sts then work: "sc2tog over last 2 sts—1 st decreased, turn."

To work a multiple dec at beg of row, sl st across sts of previous row that are to be decreased and into what will become first st of new row, work 1 ch (does NOT count as st), and then 1 sc into st at base of 1 ch (this is same st as used for last sl st). To work a multiple dec at the end of a row, simply turn the required number of sts before the end of the row, leaving the "decreased" sts unworked.

Increases

Work all increases at beg and ends of rows by working 2 sts into one st of previous row. Beg inc rows with: "1 ch (does NOT count as st), 2 sc into st at base of 1 ch—1 st increased." End inc rows with: "2 sc into last st—1 st increased, turn."

STITCH DIAGRAM

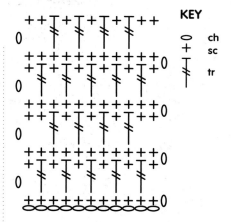

KEY

0   ch
+   sc
   tr

vest body

(worked in one piece to armholes)

With one strand of M and one strand of C held together and 7 (4.50 mm) hook, make 66 [74:82:90] ch.

1st row (RS): 1 sc into 2nd ch from hook, 1 sc into each ch to end, turn. 65 [73:81:89] sts. Now work in patt as follows:

2nd row: 1 ch (does NOT count as st), 1 sc into first sc, *1 tr into next sc, 1 sc into next sc, rep from * to end, turn.

3rd row: 1 ch (does NOT count as st), 1 sc into each st to end, turn.

4th row: 1 ch (does NOT count as st), 1 sc into each of first 2 sc, *1 tr into next sc, 1 sc into next sc, rep from * to last st, 1 sc into last st, turn.

5th row: As 3rd row.

2nd to 5th rows form patt.

Work in patt for a further 6 [8:12:16] rows, ending with WS facing for next row.

DIVIDE FOR ARMHOLES

Next row (WS): Patt first 13 [15:17:19] sts and

turn, leaving rem sts unworked.

Work on this set of 13 [15:17:19] sts only for left front.

Keeping patt correct, dec 1 st at armhole edge of next 2 [3:3:4] rows, then on foll alt row. 10 [11:13:14] sts.

Work 3 [4:2:3] rows, ending with WS facing for next row.

SHAPE NECK

Keeping patt correct, dec 2 [3:3:4] sts at front opening edge of next row. 8 [8:10:10] sts.

Dec 1 st at neck edge of next 2 rows, then on foll 1 [1:2:2] alt rows. 5 [5:6:6] sts.

Work 1 row, ending with WS facing for next row.

SHAPE SHOULDER

Fasten off.

SHAPE BACK

Return to last complete row worked before dividing for armholes, skip next 6 sts, attach yarn to next st, patt 27 [31:35:39] sts and turn, leaving rem sts unworked.

Work on this set of 27 [31:35:39] sts only for back.

Keeping patt correct, dec 1 st at each end of next 2 [3:3:4] rows, then on foll alt row. 21 [23:27:29] sts.

Work 7 [8:8:9] rows, ending with WS facing for next row.

SHAPE BACK NECK

Next row (WS): Patt first 6 [6:7:7] sts and turn, leaving rem sts unworked.

Keeping patt correct, dec 1 st at neck edge of next row, ending with WS facing for next row. 5 [5:6:6] sts.

SHAPE SHOULDER
Fasten off.

Return to last complete row worked before shaping back neck, skip next 9 [11:13:15] sts, attach yarn to next st, patt to end. 6 [6:7:7] sts.
Keeping patt correct, dec 1 st at neck edge of next row, ending with WS facing for next row. 5 [5:6:6] sts.

SHAPE SHOULDER
Fasten off.

SHAPE RIGHT FRONT
Return to last complete row worked before dividing for armholes, skip next 6 sts, attach yarn to next st, patt to end. 13 [15:17:19] sts.
Complete to match left front, reversing shapings.

Finishing

Join shoulder seams.

FRONT, HEM AND NECK BORDER
With RS facing, E4 (3.50 mm) hook and M, attach yarn to foundation ch edge directly below left armhole, 1 ch (does NOT count as st), work one round of sc evenly across hem edge, up right front opening edge, around entire neck edge, down left front opening edge and across foundation ch edge, working 3 sc into corner points and ending with sl st to first sc, turn.
Mark positions for 5 buttonholes along one front opening edge (right front for a girl, or left front for a boy)—position top buttonhole level with start of neck shaping, lowest buttonhole level with foundation ch edge of Body, and rem 3 buttonholes evenly spaced between.
Next round (WS): 1 ch (does NOT count as st), 1 sc into each sc to end, skipping sc as required around neck edge to ensure Edging lays flat, working 3 sc into corner points, making buttonholes to correspond with positions marked by replacing (1 sc into each of next 2 sc) with (2 ch, skip 2 sc), and ending with sl st to first sc, turn.
Next round: 1 ch (does NOT count as st), 1 sc into each sc to end, skipping sc as required around neck edge to ensure Edging lays flat, working 3 sc into corner points, working 2 sc into each buttonhole ch sp, and ending with sl st to first sc, do NOT turn.
Now work one round of crab st (sc worked from left to right, instead of right to left) around entire outer edge, ending with sl st to first sc.
Fasten off.

ARMHOLE BORDERS
With RS facing, E4 (3.50 mm) hook and M, attach yarn at base of armhole, 1 ch (does NOT count as st), work one round of sc evenly around entire armhole edge, ending with sl st to first sc, turn.
Next round (WS): 1 ch (does NOT count as st), 1 sc into each sc to end, sl st to first sc, turn.
Next round: 1 ch (does NOT count as st), 1 sc into each sc to end, sl st to first sc, do NOT turn.
Now work one round of crab st (sc worked from left to right, instead of right to left) around entire armhole edge, ending with sl st to first sc.
Fasten off.

Sew on buttons.

Hat

With one strand of M and one strand of C held together and 7 (4.50 mm) hook, make 42 [48:54:60] ch and join with a sl st to form a ring.

1st round (RS): 1 ch (does NOT count as st), 1 sc into each ch to end, sl st to first sc, turn. 42 [48:54:60] sts.

Now work in patt as follows:

2nd round: 1 ch (does NOT count as st), 1 sc into first sc, *1 tr into next sc**, 1 sc into next sc, rep from * to end, ending last rep at **, sl st to first sc, turn.

3rd round: 1 ch (does NOT count as st), 1 sc into each st to end, sl st to first sc, turn.

4th round: 4 ch (counts as first tr), skip st at base of 4 ch, *1 sc into next sc**, 1 tr into next sc, rep from * to end, ending last rep at **, sl st to top of 4 ch at beg of round, turn.

5th round: As 3rd round.

2nd to 5th rounds form patt.

Work in patt for a further 3 [5:5:7] rounds, ending with RS facing for next round.

SHAPE CROWN

1st round (RS): 1 ch (does NOT count as st), (sc2tog over next 2 sts, 1 sc into each of next 4 sts) 7 [8:9:10] times, sl st to first sc, turn. 35 [40:45:50] sts.

Keeping patt correct, work 1 round.

3rd round: 1 ch (does NOT count as st), (sc2tog over next 2 sts, 1 sc into each of next 3 sts) 7 [8:9:10] times, sl st to first sc, turn. 28 [32:36:40] sts.

4th round: 1 ch (does NOT count as st), (patt 2 sts, sc2tog over next 2 sts) 7 [8:9:10] times, sl st to first sc, turn. 21 [24:27:30] sts.

5th round: 1 ch (does NOT count as st), (sc2tog over next 2 sts, 1 sc into next st) 7 [8:9:10] times, sl st to first sc, turn. 14 [16:18:20] sts.

6th round: 1 ch (does NOT count as st), (sc2tog over next 2 sts) 7 [8:9:10] times, sl st to first sc, turn. 7 [8:9:10] sts.

7th round: 1 ch (does NOT count as st), (sc2tog over next 2 sts) 3 [4:4:5] times, (1 sc into last st) 1 [0:1:0] times, sl st to first sc. 4 [4:5:5] sts.

Fasten off. Run a gathering thread around top of last round of Hat, pull up tight and fasten off securely.

Finishing

LOWER BORDER

With RS facing, E4 (3.50 mm) hook and M, attach yarn to foundation ch edge, 1 ch (does NOT count as st), work one round of sc evenly around entire foundation ch edge, ending with sl st to first sc, turn.

Next round (WS): 1 ch (does NOT count as st), 1 sc into each sc to end, sl st to first sc, turn.

Next round: 1 ch (does NOT count as st), 1 sc into each sc to end, sl st to first sc, do NOT turn.

Now work one round of crab st (sc worked from left to right, instead of right to left) around entire lower edge, ending with sl st to first sc.

Fasten off.

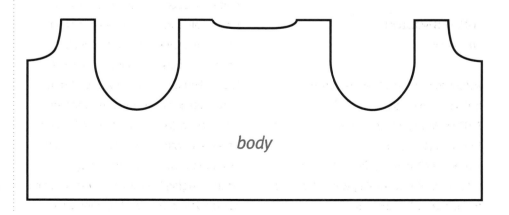

body

Boy and girl dolls

These adorable dolls are sure to delight any little one. Simply made in single crochet using a DK-weight yarn, their construction means there's very little sewing to do too! Their clothes are removable—so you could make them a whole wardrobe to wear.

MEASUREMENT
Complete Doll stands approx 12 in (30 cm) tall

MATERIALS
• Rowan RYC Cashsoft Baby DK (50 g balls): 2 balls in pink (Pixie 807) and 1 ball in each of cream (Horseradish 801) and pale orange (Imp 803)
• Rowan RYC Cashsoft DK (50 g balls): 1 ball in each of navy (Navy 514), brown (Truffle 527), red (Poppy 512) and green (Lime 509)
• Size E4 (3.50 mm) crochet hook
• Washable toy filling

ABBREVIATIONS
• loop 1—insert hook into next st, form loop of yarn around first finger of left hand (for girl doll, draw out this loop to approx 4–5 in (10–12 cm), or for boy doll approx ¾ in (2 cm) and draw both strands of this looped yarn through st, yarn over hook and draw through all 3 loops on hook. See also page 9.

GAUGE
19 stitches and 20 rows to 4 in (10 cm) measured over single crochet fabric using E4 (3.50 mm) hook.
Change hook size if necessary to obtain this gauge.

STITCH DIAGRAM

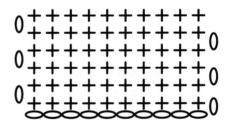

KEY
○ ch
+ sc

Doll legs *(make two)*

With E4 (3.50 mm) hook and pink, make 12 ch and join with a sl st to form a ring.

1st round (RS): 1 ch (does NOT count as st), 1 sc into each ch to end, sl st to first sc, turn. 12 sts.

2nd round: 1 ch (does NOT count as st), 1 sc into each sc to end, sl st to first sc, turn.

3rd to 18th rounds: As 2nd round.

Break off pink and join in cream.

19th to 21st rounds: As 2nd round.

Break off cream and slip working loop onto a safety pin.

These 21 rounds form leg and ankle sock section. Now work foot as follows:

Girl doll

With WS facing, skip first 4 sc of next round, rejoin cream to next st, 1 ch (does NOT count as st), 1 sc into sc where yarn was rejoined, 1 sc into each of next 3 sc, turn. 4 sts.

Next row: 1 ch (does NOT count as st), 1 sc into each sc to end, turn.

Rep last row once more, ending with RS facing for next row.

Break off cream and join in navy.

Rep last row 3 times more, ending with WS facing for next row.

Fasten off.

Boy doll

With WS facing, skip first 4 sc of next round, rejoin brown to next st, 1 ch (does NOT count as st), 1 sc into sc where yarn was rejoined, 1 sc into each of next 3 sc, turn. 4 sts.

Next row: 1 ch (does NOT count as st), 1 sc into each sc to end, turn.

Rep last row 4 times more, ending with WS facing for next row.

Fasten off.

Both dolls

Return to working loop left on safety pin and slip this loop back onto hook. With WS facing and shoe color (navy for Girl, or brown for Boy), work as follows: 1 ch (does NOT count as st), 1 sc into each of first 4 sc of last round worked before shaping foot, 5 sc evenly up row-end edge of top of foot section, 4 sc evenly across end of top of foot section, and 5 sc evenly down other row-end edge of top of foot section, then 1 sc into each of last 4 sc of last round, sl st to first sc, turn. 22 sts.

Next round: 1 ch (does NOT count as st), 1 sc into each sc to end, sl st to first sc, turn.

Rep last round twice more, ending with WS facing for next round.

Next round (WS): 1 ch (does NOT count as st), (1 sc into next sc, sc2tog over next 2 sc, 1 sc into each of next 5 sc, sc2tog over next 2 sc, 1 sc into next sc) twice, sl st to first sc, turn. 18 sts.

Next round: 1 ch (does NOT count as st), (sc2tog over next 2 sc, 1 sc into each of next 5 sc, sc2tog over next 2 sc) twice, sl st to first sc, turn. 14 sts.

Fasten off.

Fold foot section in half and join top of last round to form seam along base of foot. Insert toy filling so foot and leg are quite firmly filled. Fold top of leg flat, with start and ends of rounds at center back.

Arms *(make two)*

THUMB

With E4 (3.50 mm) hook and pink, make 3 ch.

1st round (RS): 1 sc into 2nd ch from hook, 2 sc into next ch, working back along other side of ch: 1 sc into next ch (this is same ch as used for first sc), sl st to first sc. 4 sts. Fasten off.

HAND

With E4 (3.50 mm) hook and pink, make 4 ch.

1st round (RS): 1 sc into 2nd ch from hook, 1 sc into next ch, 2 sc into last ch, working back along other side of ch: 1 sc into each of next 2 ch (2nd of these is same ch as used for first sc), sl st to first sc, turn. 6 sts.

2nd round: 1 ch (does NOT count as st), 2 sc into first sc, 1 sc into next sc, 2 sc into each of next 2 sc, 1 sc into next sc, 2 sc into last sc, sl st to first sc, turn. 10 sts.

3rd round: 1 ch (does NOT count as st), 2 sc into first sc, 1 sc into each of next 3 sc, 2 sc into each of next 2 sc, 1 sc into each of next 3 sc, 2 sc into last sc, sl st to first sc, turn. 14 sts.

4th round: 1 ch (does NOT count as st), 1 sc into each sc to end, sl st to first sc, turn.

5th round: As 4th round.

JOIN THUMB TO HAND

6th round (WS): 1 ch (does NOT count as st),

1 sc into each of first 7 sts of Hand, 1 sc into each of next 4 sc of Thumb, 1 sc into each of last 7 sts of Hand, sl st to first sc, turn. 18 sts.

Note: Where Thumb joins Hand, small hole is formed. It will be much easier to sew this hole closed now!

7th round: As 4th round.

8th round: 1 ch (does NOT count as st), 1 sc into each of first 7 sc, (sc2tog over next 2 sc) twice, 1 sc into each of last 7 sc, sl st to first sc, turn. 16 sts.

9th round: 1 ch (does NOT count as st), 1 sc into each of first 6 sc, (sc2tog over next 2 sc) twice, 1 sc into each of last 6 sc, sl st to first sc, turn. 14 sts.

10th round: 1 ch (does NOT count as st), sc2tog over first 2 sc, 1 sc into each of next 3 sc, (sc2tog over next 2 sc) twice, 1 sc into each of next 3 sc, sc2tog over last 2 sc, sl st to first sc, turn. 10 sts.

11th to 20th rounds: As 4th round.
Fasten off.

Insert toy filling so hand and arm are fairly firmly filled.

Body

BASE

With E4 (3.50 mm) hook and cream, make 14 ch.

1st row (RS): 1 sc into 2nd ch from hook, 1 sc into each ch to end, turn. 13 sts.

2nd row: 1 ch (does NOT count as st), 1 sc into each sc to end, turn.

3rd row: 1 ch (does NOT count as st), sc2tog

over first 2 sc, 1 sc into each sc to last 2 sc, sc2tog over last 2 sc, turn. 11 sts.

4th to 6th rows: As 3rd row. 5 sts.

Fasten off.

Base is a triangular shape—foundation ch edge is front edge and last row is center back edge.

BODY

With RS facing, E4 (3.50 mm) hook and cream, attach yarn at center of last row and work around Base as follows:

1st round (RS): 1 ch (does NOT count as st), work 9 sc evenly along first shaped edge to foundation ch edge, holding Legs against RS of Base, work 1 sc into each of first 6 foundation ch enclosing top folded edge of Leg in sts (make sure Foot points forwards!), 1 sc into next foundation ch, now work 1 sc into each of last 6 foundation ch enclosing top folded edge of other Leg in sts, now work 9 sc evenly along other shaped edge of Base to point where yarn was rejoined, sl st to first sc, turn. 31 sts.

2nd round: 1 ch (does NOT count as st), 1 sc into each sc to end, sl st to first sc, turn.

3rd and 4th rounds: As 2nd round.

5th round: 1 ch (does NOT count as st), 1 sc into each of first 7 sc, sc2tog over next 2 sc, 1 sc into each of next 13 sc, sc2tog over next 2 sc, 1 sc into each of last 7 sc, sl st to first sc, turn. 29 sts.

6th round: 1 ch (does NOT count as st), sc2tog over first 2 sc, 1 sc into each of next 6 sc, sc2tog over next 2 sc, 1 sc into each of next 9 sc, sc2tog over next 2 sc, 1 sc into each of next 6 sc, sc2tog over last 2 sc, sl st

to first sc, turn. 25 sts.

7th round: As 2nd round.

8th round: 1 ch (does NOT count as st), 1 sc into each of first 5 sc, sc2tog over next 2 sc, 1 sc into each of next 11 sc, sc2tog over next 2 sc, 1 sc into each of last 5 sc, sl st to first sc, turn. 23 sts.

Break off cream and join in pink.

9th round: 1 ch (does NOT count as st), sc2tog over first 2 sc, 1 sc into each of next 4 sc, sc2tog over next 2 sc, 1 sc into each of next 7 sc, sc2tog over next 2 sc, 1 sc into each of next 4 sc, sc2tog over last 2 sc, sl st to first sc, turn. 19 sts.

10th round: As 2nd round.

11th round: 1 ch (does NOT count as st), 1 sc into each of first 3 sc, sc2tog over next 2 sc, 1 sc into each of next 9 sc, sc2tog over next 2 sc, 1 sc into each of last 3 sc, sl st to first sc, turn. 17 sts.

12th round: 1 ch (does NOT count as st), sc2tog over first 2 sc, 1 sc into each of next 2 sc, sc2tog over next 2 sc, 1 sc into each of next 5 sc, sc2tog over next 2 sc, 1 sc into each of next 2 sc, sc2tog over last 2 sc, sl st to first sc, turn. 13 sts.

JOIN ARMS TO BODY

13th round: 1 ch (does NOT count as st), 1 sc into each of first 3 sc of Body, 1 sc into each of next 10 sc of first Arm, 1 sc into each of next 7 sc of Body, 1 sc into each of next 10 sc of second Arm, 1 sc into each of last 3 sc of Body, sl st to first sc, turn. 33 sts.

Note: Where Arms join Body, small holes are formed at underarm. It will be much easier to sew these holes closed now!

14th round: 1 ch (does NOT count as st), 1 sc into each of first 3 sc, sc2tog over next 2 sc, 1 sc into each of next 6 sc, sc2tog over next 2 sc, 1 sc into each of next 7 sc, sc2tog over next 2 sc, 1 sc into each of next 6 sc, sc2tog over next 2 sc, 1 sc into each of last 3 sc, sl st to first sc, turn. 29 sts.

15th round: 1 ch (does NOT count as st), 1 sc into each of first 3 sc, sc2tog over next 2 sc, 1 sc into each of next 4 sc, sc2tog over next 2 sc, 1 sc into each of next 7 sc, sc2tog over next 2 sc, 1 sc into each of next 4 sc, sc2tog over next 2 sc, 1 sc into each of last 3 sc, sl st to first sc, turn. 25 sts.

Insert toy filling so that lower section of Body is firmly filled.

16th round: 1 ch (does NOT count as st), 1 sc into each of first 3 sc, sc2tog over next 2 sc, 1 sc into each of next 2 sc, sc2tog over next 2 sc, 1 sc into each of next 7 sc, sc2tog over next 2 sc, 1 sc into each of next 2 sc, sc2tog over next 2 sc, 1 sc into each of last 3 sc, sl st to first sc, turn. 21 sts.

17th round: 1 ch (does NOT count as st), 1 sc into each of first 3 sc, (sc2tog over next 2 sc) twice, 1 sc into each of next 7 sc, (sc2tog over next 2 sc) twice, 1 sc into each of last 3 sc, sl st to first sc, turn. 17 sts.

18th round: 1 ch (does NOT count as st), 1 sc into first sc, (sc2tog over next 2 sc) 3 times, 1 sc into each of next 3 sc, (sc2tog over next 2 sc) 3 times, 1 sc into last sc, sl st to first sc, turn. 11 sts.

19th round: As 2nd round.

Fasten off.

Insert toy filling so that upper section of Body and Arms is firmly filled.

Head

With E4 (3.50 mm) hook and pink, make 11 ch and fasten off. (11 "v" shapes visible along length of ch.)

1st round (RS): attach yarn to center ch, 1 ch (does NOT count as st), 1 sc into ch where yarn was rejoined, 1 sc into each of next 4 ch, 2 sc into last ch, now working back along other side of foundation ch: 1 sc into same ch as last 2 sc, 1 sc into each of next 10 ch (last of these sc is worked into last ch), now working back along rem edge of foundation ch: 2 sc into same place as last sc, 1 sc into each of next 4 ch, 1 sc into same ch as sc at beg of round, sl st to first sc, turn. 25 sts.

2nd round: 1 ch (does NOT count as st), 1 sc into each of first 6 sc, 2 sc into each of next 2 sc, 1 sc into each of next 9 sc, 2 sc into each of next 2 sc, 1 sc into each of last 6 sc, sl st to first sc, turn. 29 sts.
Now working in rows, not rounds, cont as follows:

3rd row: 1 ch (does NOT count as st), sc2tog over first 2 sc, 1 sc into each of next 5 sc, 2 sc into each of next 2 sc, 1 sc into each of next 11 sc, 2 sc into each of next 2 sc, 1 sc into each of next 5 sc, sc2tog over next 2 sc, turn. 31 sts.

4th row: 1 ch (does NOT count as st), sc2tog over first 2 sc, 1 sc into each of next 5 sc, 2 sc into each of next 2 sc, 1 sc into each of next 13 sc, 2 sc into each of next 2 sc, 1 sc into each of next 5 sc, sc2tog over next 2 sc, turn. 33 sts.

5th row: 1 ch (does NOT count as st), 1 sc into each sc to end, turn.

6th row: 1 ch (does NOT count as st), 1 sc into each of first 7 sc, 2 sc into next sc, 1 sc into each of next 17 sc, 2 sc into next sc, 1 sc into each of last 7 sc, turn. 35 sts.

7th row: As 5th row.
Now working in rounds, not rows, cont as follows:

8th round: 1 ch (does NOT count as st), 2 sc into first sc, 1 sc into each sc to last sc, 2 sc into last sc, sl st to first sc, turn. 37 sts.

9th round: 1 ch (does NOT count as st), 1 sc into each sc to end, sl st to first sc, turn.

10th round: 1 ch (does NOT count as st), sc2tog over first 2 sc, 1 sc into each sc to last 2 sc, sc2tog over last 2 sc, sl st to first sc, turn. 35 sts.
Fasten off.
Skip first 9 sts of next round, rejoin yarn to next sc and complete front of Head as follows:

11th row (RS): 1 ch (does NOT count as st), sc2tog over sc where yarn was rejoined and next sc, 1 sc into each of next 13 sc, sc2tog over next 2 sc and turn, leaving rem 9 sts unworked. 15 sts.

12th row: As 5th row.

13th row: 1 ch (does NOT count as st), sc2tog over first 2 sc, 1 sc into each sc to last 2 sc, sc2tog over last 2 sc, turn. 13 sts.

14th to 16th rows: As 13th row. 7 sts.
Fasten off.

Hair

With E4 (3.50 mm) hook and hair color (pale orange for girl doll, or brown for boy doll), make 2 ch.

1st round (RS): 6 sc into 2nd ch from hook, sl st to first sc, turn. 6 sts.

2nd round: 1 ch (does NOT count as st), (loop 1) twice into each sc to end, sl st to first st, turn. 12 sts.

3rd round: 1 ch (does NOT count as st), (2 sc into next st, 1 sc into next st) 6 times, sl st to first sc, turn. 18 sts.

4th round: 1 ch (does NOT count as st), loop 1 into each sc to end, sl st to first st, turn.

5th round: 1 ch (does NOT count as st), (2 sc into next st, 1 sc into next st) 9 times, sl st to first sc, turn. 27 sts.

6th round: As 4th round.

7th round: 1 ch (does NOT count as st), 1 sc into first st, (2 sc into next st, 1 sc into next st) 13 times, sl st to first sc, turn. 40 sts.

8th round: As 4th round.

9th round: 1 ch (does NOT count as st), (2 sc into next st, 1 sc into next st) 20 times, sl st to first sc, turn. 60 sts.

10th round: As 4th round.
Fasten off.

Sew outer edge of Hair section to top of Head. Insert toy filling so Head is firmly filled, then sew neck opening of Head to top of Body, inserting a little more toy filling into neck section.

Finishing

Using photograph as a guide, embroider french knot eyes using navy and french knot mouth using red. Carefully snip each "loop 1" of hair section to create shaggy hair-like effect.

For girl doll, cut a double length of navy yarn and thread through foot and tie ends in a bow on top of foot as in photograph.

GIRL'S HAIR BOW

With E4 (3.50 mm) hook and red, make 18 ch and join with a sl st to form a ring.

1st round (RS): 1 ch (does NOT count as st), 1 sc into each of first 2 ch, 1 dc into each of next 6 ch, 1 sc into each of next 3 ch, 1 dc into each of next 6 ch, 1 sc into last ch, sl st to first sc, do NOT turn. 18 sts.

2nd round: Skip st at base of sl st closing last round, 1 sl st into next sc, 1 dc into each of next 6 dc, 1 sl st into each of next 3 sc, 1 dc into each of next 6 dc, 1 sl st into last sc. Fasten off, leaving a long end.

Wrap this long end round center of bow several times and secure end. Attach bow to top of head as in photograph.

Boy's shorts

FIRST LEG: With E4 (3.50 mm) hook and navy, make 21 ch and join with a sl st to form a ring.

1st round (RS): 1 ch (does NOT count as st), 1 sc into each ch to end, sl st to first sc, turn. 21 sts.

2nd round: 1 ch (does NOT count as st), 1 sc into each sc to end, sl st to first sc, turn.

3rd to 8th rounds: As 2nd round.

9th round: 1 ch (does NOT count as st), 2 sc into first sc, 1 sc into each of next 7 sc, sc2tog over next 2 sc, 1 sc into next

sc, sc2tog over next 2 sc, 1 sc into each of next 7 sc, 2 sc into last sc, sl st to first sc, turn. 21 sts.

10th round: As 2nd round.

Fasten off.

SECOND LEG: Work as given for First Leg to end of 10th round.

Do NOT fasten off.

JOIN LEGS

11th round (RS): 1 ch (does NOT count as st), work 1 sc into each sc of Second Leg, then work 1 sc into each sc of First Leg, sl st to first sc, turn. 42 sts.

Note: Where Legs join, small hole is formed. It will be much easier to sew this hole closed now!

12th round: 1 ch (does NOT count as st), sc2tog over first 2 sc, 1 sc into each of next 17 sc, (sc2tog over next 2 sc) twice, 1 sc into each of next 17 sc, sc2tog over next 2 sc, sl st to first sc, turn. 38 sts.

13th round: 1 ch (does NOT count as st), sc2tog over first 2 sc, 1 sc into each of next 15 sc, (sc2tog over next 2 sc) twice, 1 sc into each of next 15 sc, sc2tog over next 2 sc, sl st to first sc, turn. 34 sts.

14th to 19th rounds: As 2nd round.

20th round: 1 ch (does NOT count as st), (sc2tog over next 2 sc, 1 sc into each of next 4 sc, sc2tog over next 2 sc, 1 sc into next sc, sc2tog over next 2 sc, 1 sc into each of next 4 sc, sc2tog over next 2 sc) twice, sl st to first sc, turn. 26 sts.

21st round: As 2nd round.

Fasten off.

Girl's skirt

With E4 (3.50 mm) hook and red, make 60 ch and join with a sl st to form a ring.

1st round (RS): 1 ch (does NOT count as st), 1 sc into each ch to end, sl st to first sc, turn. 60 sts.

2nd round: 1 ch (does NOT count as st), 1 sc into each sc to end, sl st to first sc, turn.

3rd round: 1 ch (does NOT count as st), (1 sc into each of next 4 sc, sc2tog over next 2 sc, 1 sc into each of next 4 sc) 6 times, sl st to first sc, turn. 54 sts.

4th to 6th rounds: As 2nd round.

7th round: 1 ch (does NOT count as st), (1 sc into each of next 3 sc, sc2tog over next 2 sc, 1 sc into each of next 4 sc) 6 times, sl st to first sc, turn. 48 sts.

8th to 10th rounds: As 2nd round.

11th round: 1 ch (does NOT count as st), (1 sc into each of next 3 sc, sc2tog over next 2 sc, 1 sc into each of next 3 sc) 6 times, sl st to first sc, turn. 42 sts.

12th and 13th rounds: As 2nd round.

14th round: 1 ch (does NOT count as st), (1 sc into each of next 2 sc, sc2tog over next 2 sc, 1 sc into each of next 3 sc) 6 times, sl st to first sc, turn. 36 sts.

15th and 16th rounds: As 2nd round.

17th round: 1 ch (does NOT count as st), (1 sc into each of next 2 sc, sc2tog over next 2 sc, 1 sc into each of next 2 sc) 6 times, sl st to first sc, turn. 30 sts.

18th and 19th rounds: As 2nd round.

20th round: 1 ch (does NOT count as st), (1 sc into next sc, sc2tog over next 2 sc, 1 sc into each of next 2 sc) 6 times, sl st to first sc, turn. 24 sts.

21st round: As 2nd round.

Fasten off.

Using photograph as a guide, embroider lines of chain stitch around lower edge of skirt in navy and green.

Boy's sweater

SLEEVES

With E4 (3.50 mm) hook and red, make 14 ch and join with a sl st to form a ring.

1st round (RS): 1 ch (does NOT count as st), 1 sc into each ch to end, sl st to first sc, turn. 14 sts.

2nd round: 1 ch (does NOT count as st), 1 sc into each sc to end, sl st to first sc, turn. Join in green.

Working next 2 rounds using green, then continuing in stripes of 2 rounds in each color, cont as follows:

3rd to 10th rounds: As 2nd round.

Fasten off.

BODY

With E4 (3.50 mm) hook and green, make 32 ch and join with a sl st to form a ring.

1st round (RS): 1 ch (does NOT count as st), 1 sc into each ch to end, sl st to first sc, turn. 32 sts.

2nd round: 1 ch (does NOT count as st), 1 sc into each sc to end, sl st to first sc, turn.

Join in red.

Working next 2 rounds using red, then continuing in stripes of 2 rounds in each

color, cont as follows:

3rd to 5th rounds: As 2nd round.

6th round: 1 ch (does NOT count as st), 1 sc into each of first 6 sc, (sc2tog over next 2 sc) twice, 1 sc into each of next 12 sc, (sc2tog over next 2 sc) twice, 1 sc into each of last 6 sc, sl st to first sc, turn. 28 sts.

7th and 8th rounds: As 2nd round.

JOIN SLEEVES TO BODY

Keeping stripes correct and now working in rows, not rounds, cont as follows:

1st row (RS): 1 ch (does NOT count as st), 1 sc into each of first 5 sc of Body, sc2tog over next 2 sc, work around 14 sc of first Sleeve as follows: *sc2tog over first 2 sc, 1 sc into each of next 10 sc, sc2tog over last 2 sc*, work across next 14 sc of Body as follows: sc2tog over next 2 sc, 1 sc into each of next 10 sc, sc2tog over next 2 sc, work around 14 sc of second Sleeve in same way as for first Sleeve (by working from * to *), then work across rem 7 sc of Body as follows: sc2tog over next 2 sc, 1 sc into each of last 5 sc, turn. 48 sts.

Note: Where Sleeves join Body, small holes are formed at underarm. It will be much easier to sew these holes closed now!

2nd row: 1 ch (does NOT count as st), * 1 sc into each of next 4 sc, (sc2tog over next 2 sc) twice, 1 sc into each of next 8 sc, (sc2tog over next 2 sc) twice, 1 sc into each of next 4 sc, rep from * once more, turn. 40 sts.

3rd row: 1 ch (does NOT count as st), (1 sc into each of next 5 sc, sc2tog over next

2 sc, 1 sc into each of next 6 sc, sc2tog over next 2 sc, 1 sc into each of next 5 sc) twice, turn. 36 sts.

4th row: 1 ch (does NOT count as st), (1 sc into each of next 5 sc, sc2tog over next 2 sc, 1 sc into each of next 4 sc, sc2tog over next 2 sc, 1 sc into each of next 5 sc) twice, turn. 32 sts.

5th row: 1 ch (does NOT count as st), (1 sc into each of next 5 sc, sc2tog over next 2 sc, 1 sc into each of next 2 sc, sc2tog over next 2 sc, 1 sc into each of next 5 sc) twice, turn. 28 sts.

6th row: 1 ch (does NOT count as st), *1 sc into each of next 5 sc, (sc2tog over next 2 sc) twice, 1 sc into each of next 5 sc, rep from * once more, turn. 24 sts.

7th row: 1 ch (does NOT count as st), (1 sc into each of next 5 sc, sc2tog over next 2 sc, 1 sc into each of next 5 sc) twice, turn. 22 sts.

8th row: 1 ch (does NOT count as st), (1 sc into each of next 3 sc, sc2tog over next 2 sc, 1 sc into next sc, sc2tog over next 2 sc, 1 sc into each of next 3 sc) twice, turn. 18 sts.

Do NOT fasten off but slip working loop onto a safety pin.

Put Sweater onto Doll, slip hook back into working loop and close back neck opening by working sl st to first sc, fasten off.

Girl's sweater

Work as given for Boy's Sweater but using green throughout.

Index

Yarn suppliers

ROWAN & JAEGER (US)
Westminster Fibers Inc
165 Ledge Street
Nashua
NH 03063
Tel: (603) 886 5041/5043
www.westminsterfibers.com

ROWAN & JAEGER (UK)
Rowan
Green Lane Mill
Holmfirth
West Yorks HD9 2DX
Tel: 44 (0)1484 681881
www.knitrowan.com

ROWAN & JAEGER (Canada)
Diamond Yarn (Canada),
155 Martin Ross, Unit 3,
Toronto M3J 2L9
Ontario
Tel: (416) 736 1111
www.diamondyarn.com

COLINETTE YARNS LTD (US)
Unique Kolours
28 N. Bacton Hill Road
Malvern
Pennsylvania 19355
Tel: (610) 644-4885

COLINETTE YARNS LTD (UK)
Banwy Workshops
Llanfair Caereinion
SY21 0SG
Wales
Tel: 44 (0)1938 810128
Fax: 44 (0)1938 810127
www.colinette.co.uk

TWILLEYS OF STAMFORD
Roman Mill
Stamford
PE9 1BG
Tel: 44 (0)1780 752661
Fax: 44 (0)1780 765215
Email: twilleys@tbramsden.co.uk
www.twilleys.co.uk

STANDARD YARN WEIGHT SYSTEM

Categories of yarn, gauge ranges, and recommended hook sizes from the Craft Yarn Council of America.
YarnStandards.com

	1 SUPER FINE	2 FINE	3 LIGHT	4 MEDIUM	5 BULKY	6 SUPER BULKY
Yarnweight Symbol and Cateory Names						
Types of Yarns in Category	Sock, Fingering, Baby	Sport, Baby	DK, Light Worsted	Worsted, Afgan, Aran	Chunky, Craft, Rug	Bulky, Roving
Crochet Gauge* Ranges in Single Crochet to 4 in (10 cm)	21–32 sts	16–20 sts	12–17 sts	11–14 sts	8–11 sts	5–9 sts
Recommended Hook in Metric Size Range	2.25–3.5mm	3.5–4.5mm	4.5–5.5mm	5.5–6.5mm	6.5–9mm	9mm and larger
Recommended Hook in U.S. Size Range	B-1 to E-4	E-4 to 7	7 to I-9	I-9 to K-10½	K-10½ to M-13	M-13 and larger

* GUIDELINES ONLY: The above reflect the most commonly used gauges and hook sizes